10 Most Common Mistakes Dog Owners Make

And How to Resolve Them

Tammie Rogers

© 2017 Tammie Rogers

All rights reserved.

ISBN-13: 978-1548482794
ISBN-10: 154848279X

Library of Congress Control Number: 2017914318
CreateSpace Independent Publishing Platform, North Charleston, SC

To Breeze.
Of all the dogs I have had the privilege to love, he taught me that what I may initially perceive as a weakness is often a dog's greatest strength. Perspective is everything.

Contents

	Acknowledgments	i
	Author's Note	iv
1	Don't versus Do	1
2	The Four Steps of Socialization	6
3	The Ten Mistakes	16
	#1: Skimpy Standards	17
	#2: Presenting Poor Presence	25
	#3: Permitting Pulling	36
	#4: Dedicated to Desensitizing	49
	#5: Tolerating Teeth	58
	#6: Missing Management	65
	#7: Misguided Methods	71
	#8: Suspecting Sabotage	83
	#9: Tenderness before Trust	90
	#10: Shortsighted Selection	96
4	Beyond the Top Ten	113
5	Wrap It Up	118
	Appendix A: Tools	121
	Appendix B: Training Methods	122
	Appendix C: Breed Selection	133
	Appendix D: Breeder Research	142

Acknowledgments

Robert—my pillar of strength and encouragement—words are not enough to express my gratitude.

To all our clients who have trusted us with their precious dogs and believed in our process to help them create the best relationship with their pups—thank you.

Author's Note

While the examples in this book are authentic, I have changed names and identifying characteristics, like the dog's breed or gender. I have modified some of the details regarding clients, but the general premise of each illustration is accurate. Also, it must be noted that while I share my thoughts on how to resolve some of the most common mistakes that dog owners make, this book is not intended as a how-to manual for dog training. Any dog that presents with antisocial behavior, especially aggression, should be seen in person by a trained professional for assistance.

1
Don't versus Do

My brain was struggling to catch up with my body as I raced from my office. When I got to the kitchen, I acknowledged that I was running toward the sound of a puppy in peril. By the time I entered the laundry room, I had gauged the severity of the screaming. I was going to find a puppy that was dangling, perhaps with its toe caught in the wire gate, ripping flesh off its precious little foot. I hoped it would be only that—although that seemed horrific enough. The shrieking was rhythmic, about a howl per second. I could hear the labored inhale between each cry.

At the far side of the laundry room was my destination. It was four feet wide by eight feet long with two-foot-high plywood sides. The scent of cedar shavings wafted my way. I tripped over a laundry basket and then zigzagged around a dog crate to reach my target. There were seven of them: darling little Border Collie babies in the whelping pen. They had just turned five weeks old. I was hoping that there would still be seven healthy puppies after I addressed the shrieking pup's trauma.

I inhaled deeply and then exhaled. It felt as if this were the first breath I'd taken since being catapulted from my office. At the far end of the pen was the puppy in question. He was not hanging, caught, or otherwise trapped in any way. He was not bleeding. He was situated as deeply into the corner as he could manage. His spine was pressed against that plywood box as if he were being sucked into it by an external force. His head was pulled back into his chest. This caused his right front foot to lift slightly off the ground, and it vibrated with each repetitive wail.

After an initial assessment, I cocked my head. Then

I permitted myself to move my investigation away from the puppy. In the absolute opposite corner of the whelping pen lay his mama. Lexie was a beautiful dog, with perfect Border Collie markings and a kind disposition to match. She was a very special dog and the daughter of my first Border Collie—who had changed the trajectory of my life forever. Lexie had whelped her litter a few weeks earlier. In doing so, she might have donated calcium from her own bones to support the growth of her babies. She had given up her routine, easy life to tend to little animals that depended upon her for nearly every life function. If something had been seriously wrong with that bellowing puppy, she would surely have acted more alarmed.

Instead, Lexie displayed the demeanor of a princess diva. I could almost detect a flick of her head away from that pup, as if to intentionally disregard his drama. She was clearly snubbing the babe. All the while, he was near the point of hyperventilating. His eyes were as big as saucers. His ears were plastered so tightly against his head that he looked like a bald old man. I wondered what might have happened.

Just then, I saw another puppy get up and move toward her mother. At five weeks, the puppies could walk, but at times, they still looked a bit drunk. When she was within a few feet of her mama, the pup dropped to her belly. Then, she displayed a very peculiar behavior: she army-crawled closer, slowly and deliberately. Lexie curled her lip nearly imperceptibly—a subtle cue that could easily go unnoticed, especially to an untrained eye. The little puppy slumped to the ground and put her chin down, looking defeated. She crawled just a few inches closer and rested her head on Lexie's paw. It was obvious that the puppy simply wanted to cuddle with her mother, but Lexie was drawing a line in the sand (or shavings, as the case was). The little female puppy had already learned her lesson. If mama curls her lip, she doesn't want you to nurse.

When puppies are born, they are blind, deaf, and unable to regulate their body temperature. They even need their mother to stimulate them to have bowel movements. They are completely dependent upon their dam. Puppies have one agenda in life at that time: to nurse. They are nipple-seeking missiles. They latch on and don't let go until they are satiated. Then they fall asleep. When they are very young, their mother is highly dedicated to keeping the puppies close, because they need her warmth. But now it was time for weaning. Imagine how traumatic it must have been for this wee, howling puppy when he discovered that everything he had ever known had been shattered.

One redeeming quality of the weaning process is that it is the most important lesson puppies ever learn. This very simple process is the foundation of canine communication. Weaning is a tutorial for dogs to remain happy and accepted in social groups for the rest of their lives. They will use it to avoid negative consequences and to prevent antisocial dogs from harassing them.

Sadly, the baby puppy that I found bawling in the whelping pen had taken that first lesson quite badly. All puppies are different; they don't all carry on the way this sniveling one did. Perhaps he was a sensitive sort of guy. Maybe his mother had been a bit heavy-handed in teaching him that nursing was no longer a free-for-all. She would now establish when the puppies could suckle—or, more accurately, when they could *not* dine. This distinction is critical to understand and assimilate: dogs rarely tell others what *to* do. Their communication is designed to express what behavior is *not* acceptable.

This book is about the mistakes that dog owners often make. At the core of the most common errors is the ideology that it is our job to manipulate the dog and to teach him what *to* do. And this goes against all that is canine. Dogs do not dedicate energy to telling other dogs what to do, and they do not inhibit them. They permit other dogs their free will and expect them to exhibit self-restraint. Higher-ranking ones are responsible for establishing clear boundaries. The younger dogs then live within those limits or deal with the consequences of noncompliance. Dogs don't tether other dogs to manage or restrain them. Nor do they use a vending-machine strategy of doling out a constant supply of bribes for agreeable behavior. They set rules, observe, forewarn, and then deliver corrections if necessary.

Certainly, teaching dogs to *do* tasks is part of dog ownership; however, most people do not struggle to train their pets to do a trick or even get the dog to sit or lie down on a verbal or signal command. I hear it all the time: "Joey knows 'sit,' 'down,' 'shake paw,' and 'roll over.'"

What most of my clients struggle with is bad manners—like jumping up, pulling on the leash, barking, whining, and biting. These are behaviors that we want to extinguish. Folks may be able to teach their dogs to sit, but they fail at establishing the standard of staying in place. I see no value in a dog that will sit on command but won't stay put! Sit must include stay.

Remaining in position is really about not getting up. It falls under the category of *don't* rather than *do*. It should be taught in a similar method as teaching a dog not to pull on the leash or to nip at our hands. It can be accomplished in the same way that Lexie taught her baby that she would determine dinnertime, not he.

If we are going to ask our dogs to integrate into our lives, learn a verbal language, and deal with our crazy human mannerisms, then we should do our best to use dog-friendly methods to communicate our expectations. This means that we need to shift our strategy from teaching dogs what *to do* and learn how to communicate what behaviors to *avoid*. Addressing the most common mistakes that dog owners make indicates how we should invert our usual philosophy.

Dogs and humans are able to cohabitate for a number of reasons, including the fact that dogs have been domesticated and artificially bred to present behaviors we find useful. I believe that dogs and humans get on so well because we are both social species that appoint guidelines for our society members and demand a level of behavior that makes living in the society better than living alone. We value cohabitating with others who are respectful of the boundaries we set—both humans and dogs.

For that reason, we can forge the finest relationships with our dogs and encourage the best behavior from them by acknowledging and supporting their canine strategy for social conduct. The good thing is that we are already equipped to do so—we can focus on what we already know, but we can also make the necessary adjustments to accommodate some clear differences between our species.

By highlighting these top ten mistakes, I hope to enlighten and encourage you to always recall the fundamental needs of your dog as a domestic, social species. This will generate the best opportunity to overcome your mistakes and live a happy and more enriching life with your dog.

2
The Four Steps of Socialization

This book is not intended to be a how-to guide of dog training and socialization. I have written other books that cover those topics in great detail (see Appendix). However, a dependable and compassionate relationship with your dog is built on some very important socialization foundations, and you must understand them if you are to resolve several of the common mistakes I identify in this book.

Lexie, as described in the previous chapter, communicated her expectations to her puppies in a four-step process. First, she set a standard: she would decide if a puppy could suckle. Second, she paid attention. There was no point in having a standard if she didn't watch to make certain that a puppy didn't slither in for a drink when she was not ready to open the bar, so to speak.

Next, if she saw a puppy moving toward the boundary she had set, she gave a warning. A warning is typically a visual or auditory cue. Common dog-warning signals include a lip curl, lowered head, change in ear set, or a low, almost unperceivable growl. We humans can use appropriately spoken words as our warnings.

The last step in the process required delivering a correction if a pup did not heed the warning. In Lexie's case, she snapped at the pup. This is typically a very quick in-and-out jab directed at the face or neck. It's swift, and there is no residual negative energy associated with the reprimand. Most people who have observed two or more dogs interacting have probably seen this action. It's the most common way that one dog creates limits for behavior when dealing with a dog that may not have the social skills to remain respectful at all times. The quick jabbing or popping touch is what a dog's nervous system processes as a correction. A grabbing, dragging, pressing, or smashing sort of contact is not perceived as a correction. A dog identifies these actions as irritating, pestering, excessive force or nagging, and these actions often do not cease the unacceptable behavior. Therefore, it is imperative that the actual physical sensation you deliver to a dog is equivalent to the sort of snap that a higher-ranking dog would inflict on a wayward pup.

The unfortunate thing is that a puppy cannot possibly know the meaning of a warning signal the first time it is offered: a curled lip or a growl has no significance until it is paired with the negative physical effect of the snap. In human terms, this is similar to telling a toddler that something is hot when he has never been burned. If such a correction is executed properly the first time, it is sufficiently unpleasant to cause learning. And it is not damaging enough to cause physical harm. If learning takes place at the first instance, then the pup does not need to be touched again. Instead, the dog will demonstrate self-restraint and avoid receiving a second jab by terminating the behavior at the warning stage.

Later, when the puppies are introduced to other dogs, they can use the lesson learned during weaning to assimilate into the family. For example, if they hear a growl when moving toward an old, grumpy dog, they can retreat before receiving an adverse consequence. If they attempt to steal another dog's bone, they will be warned—and then corrected only if they don't back away and respect the senior. The method requires a higher-ranking individual who is willing to communicate the lines in the sand that may not be crossed. But it is the offender's responsibility to use the information to change his or her behavior. It is an approach based on encouraging self-control; then there is no need to actively control a pup. This is why we seldom see dogs using leashes with their youngsters.

Four Steps to Socialization
1. Set the standard
2. Pay attention
3. Give a warning (if an offender is about to breach the standard)
4. Give a correction (if the offender did not heed the warning)

Remarkably, our own human societies have been designed with the same process. Our regulations, for the most part, do not focus on what a citizen can do. Instead, they are designed to define actions that are not acceptable. We don't have laws that say you may establish a pizza parlor, but we do have laws that say that a pizza parlor may not use expired cheese, employ child labor, or stay open past midnight.

Our laws *set standards* for socially acceptable behavior, and then we *pay attention* to citizens in various ways. The health department may visit your pizza parlor to make sure you are not using expired products. We set *warnings*—like speed-limit signs. If you fail to heed them and adjust your behavior accordingly, society *corrects* you with (generally) appropriate consequences. You might get fined for speeding, but you could serve jail time if you hurt somebody.

Once a dog has been taught what is not acceptable, we can train it to perform specific actions. When we want a dog to present a behavior on command, we should use a method designed to reinforce the behavior. That would be an appropriate time to employ positive-reinforcement techniques. Coined by B. F. Skinner, a psychologist best known as a behaviorist, "positive" here doesn't mean "pleasant." It just means "added." In other words, positive reinforcement is adding something to the lesson that strengthens the behavior.

If you give a dog a treat when she sits, you have added something (the treat) that strengthens (reinforces) the sitting behavior. I am a strong advocate of positive reinforcement for helping dogs repeat a desirable behavior. I call this strategy the *incentive method* because it offers incentives to increase the chance that the dog will repeat the behavior.

However, I do not recall ever seeing dogs using such an incentive method with each other. As I've noted, dogs tend to teach other dogs about behaviors that are not acceptable. I refer to this as *social compliance*. The concept of good manners falls under this category.

In my experience, most of the common errors that dog owners make are associated with antisocial behaviors. By "antisocial," I do not mean to imply that a dog is not friendly. Most of us have met a big, friendly dog that has jammed his nose in our crotch, jumped on us, or dragged us over, all the while wagging his tail with glee. He's friendly, but he is antisocial: he doesn't understand how to behave in a socially compliant manner. In a socially balanced group of dogs, the lower-ranking ones learn that it is not acceptable to enter the personal space of their betters. An expectation is established—in this case, "Do not enter the personal space of another dog." Then, if the junior dog begins to move toward jumping on a senior dog, a warning is issued. If the junior dog doesn't change his behavior at that point, a consequence is delivered. It must be sufficiently unpleasant to change the dog's behavior—hopefully for a long time (or forever). That is how dogs do it.

Some folks prefer an exclusively positive-reinforcement method; they teach a dog to perform a desired behavior, such as sit, for which it receives a reward. Then, if the dog begins to disrespectfully jump on someone, the handler commands the dog to perform the sit behavior. The hope is that the dog will refrain from jumping to get the reward for sitting on command—a behavior it has already learned and practiced. Of course, the question is whether the dog finds more value in jumping up or getting a treat for sitting on command. If the dog isn't hungry or is experiencing more motivation to jump, then the process fails and the dog jumps up.

Dogs do not teach their pups to perform alternate behaviors using positive reinforcement, which is essentially a swap-out strategy to alleviate a naughty behavior. They use the four-step process of socialization. I believe that we too should use this social-compliance method for eliminating bad behavior because that is what dogs do. Yes, we should add a positive-reinforcement method to create good behaviors too. I consider the combination a balanced approach to training.

As I move through the top ten lists of mistakes, I will offer additional details on how to apply the social-compliance method. It is the most dog-friendly model we can use to educate our pets about whether we accept a specific behavior in our family and society. It is also the most successful, typically the quickest, and the easiest for our beloved dogs to understand. We need to speak their language. When we do, we can significantly reduce the typical errors that most dog owners make. Above all, it is the fairest and kindest way to communicate with the unique species that we call the dog.

Pitfalls of the Social-Compliance Method: Don't Be a Jerker

I must say one vital thing about social compliance

before we move on. Although activists have pushed for twenty-five years to inflict an all-positive-reinforcement strategy on us and our dogs, many, including myself, acknowledge the value of consequence-based training. We understand the importance of correction to communicate that a dog's behavior is unacceptable. That is a good thing. However, many owners who use corrections are either off on their timing or simply omit the most important part of the process, making it less effective or even detrimental. I want to address these gaps in technique.

Some handlers mistakenly deliver the correction before giving the warning. Alternatively, they fail to give the warning all together. To me, their dogs have an inner dialog that goes something like this:

> I have a nice owner. She's pretty, she feeds me, and she gives me affection. Sometimes she even throws the ball for me. But, she is a jerker. If she is upset with me, she jerks me. I never really know why, but just out of the blue, she jerks my collar. If she wants me to go left, she doesn't say, "Let's go left." No, she just jerks me to the left. If she would just give me a little warning, it would be so much easier for me to please her. Sometimes I think that I did right, but I still get jerked. I really don't understand my owner—so I no longer pay any attention to her. I prefer to simply look around the environment to see what's out there.

If the dog is not on a leash, you might replace the word "jerk" with "yell," as in, "I have a yeller for an owner. If she is upset with me, she yells at me. I never really know why."

The goal of a correction method is to eliminate the need for corrections as soon as possible. That cannot happen if you don't put the steps in the right order. In most situations, you must offer the warning word before you deliver the correction.

More important than even the timing is whether you actually need to correct the dog. In most situations, you must not deliver the correction if your dog heeds the warning and changes his behavior. This is a vital advantage of the method.

Let's look at a very simple example of correction-based training. Because more neighborhoods these days prohibit traditional fencing, some homeowners use underground fence systems to secure their dogs. The perimeter is usually set with a buried wire; wireless models send signals from a base location. Pet collars are fitted with sensors that detect the perimeter and beep when they near it (say, at ten feet). If the collar continues to move toward the perimeter, it delivers a low-level shock that doesn't hurt the animal but discourages it from nearing the perimeter.

These electronic collars follow the four steps. The *standard* is, "Do not cross the perimeter of the yard." The system *pays attention* to the movements of the animal. The collars *beep* to give a warning, and the *correction*, if needed, is a mild shock.

To train a dog to this system, walk it on a leash at first for control over the situation. Most of my clients who have used these systems report that their dogs only required one or two corrections to understand the concept. When puppies are weaned, their mother doesn't need to snap at them repeatedly. It should be noted that the collars' beeping sound is not emotional in tone, and they never correct before a warning tone— or if the dog complies with the warning.

The intention of correction-based training is not a lifetime of corrections but to have a dog change behavior at the warning-signal stage. Warnings are ideally spoken calmly, and the dog is to change behavior upon hearing the caution words. In fact, there should be no need for a collar or leash. After all, dogs do not use collars and leashes when teaching their pups. However, they are much more observant and far quicker than we humans, so collar and leash are typically critical for initial training success.

It is important, however, to comprehend that the *tool*, like a collar or leash, is not the *method*. The method is to encourage the dog to develop self-restraint; the dog feels that he is in control of his own destiny. For that reason, a dog that is educated using the four steps of the social-compliance method develops confidence and a high regard for his owner. However, again, the handler must present the training steps in the correct order (warn before correct), and a dog that demonstrates self-restraint should not receive a correction. This is where the real learning happens: when the dog changes his behavior and does not receive a correction. That is when the dog perceives the owner as a prominent person who shares information about how he can avoid negative consequences. Regardless of what mistake a dog makes, if this method is used to resolve the issue, it must be presented accurately to the dog. That is only fair and reasonable.

Dogs are not a species whose members can exist alone in nature very well. They were designed by humans (at times, it seems, in their image), created to please their human leaders—including with some very radical behaviors, like relinquishing a freshly killed duck to a hunter, even if the dog is hungry. It includes protecting a shepherd's sheep and scavenging for its own meals but refraining from eating a newborn lamb. There are dozens of examples that reiterate the subordination of dog to human. This is a dog's genetic fate. Dogs want to please their people; they cannot escape that destiny. Some breeds are motivated to please at a higher level than others, but most domestic dogs have a heritable drive to partner with and subordinate to humans. It is vital to have a clear understanding of this strange phenomenon that exists in dogs—and no other species on the planet. The dog is not a wild animal like a dolphin that can be somewhat tamed to engage with humans when it so pleases. Dogs are a product of artificially manipulated genetics from which they cannot escape. To disregard this important information is unreasonable and unfair.

There's a final potential pitfall that needs to be mentioned before we continue. If you are someone who doesn't want your dog to be obedient, then you may find the strategies presented in this book unpleasant. Obedience is based on the premise of "because I said so." If that phrase triggers you to shudder in your boots, you should probably get a cat. Dogs need you to establish the rules so that they can strive to please you. They can become confused, frustrated, belligerent, worried, overzealous, or even aggressive if they do not receive clear information about how they are expected to behave in the society or family structure. Someone has to be responsible for imparting the rules. That person must assume the role of authority figure—the one who proclaims, "Because I said so." It's critical to understand that a leader remains calmly confident. An effective dog owner is not harsh, domineering, spiteful, loud, physically extreme, or uncaring. But he or she must take charge.

I do not intend to debunk the idea of using a positive-reinforcement-only method to train a dog. I also do not intend to tell anyone that he or she does not have the right to use such a method; however, I do strongly argue against trainers using the term "dog obedience" to mean a method based on an all-positive-reinforcement strategy.

Obedience has a very specific meaning. It is a system in which lower-ranking individuals follow the standards set by higher-ranking individuals. Most trainers who promote a positive-reinforcement-only method are staunchly opposed to the concept of actual obedience, yet they often use the term on websites to market to potential clients. The concept of "because I said so" is imperative to dog obedience. If you are reading this book because you have a dog that is presenting behaviors that frustrate you, you probably feel that the dog is not respecting your authority, even if you have not specifically used those words to describe the situation. If you are still uncomfortable with the idea of assuming the leadership role over your dog, then regardless of what I say in the remainder of this book, you may not be able to resolve your issues. On the other hand, if you are open to the idea of accepting accountability for what I often call the "parent" role to your dog, then your troubles will be answered. Read on.

The Ten Mistakes

This chapter is dedicated to presenting the most common mistakes that I believe dog owners make, with suggestions for resolving the problems.

#1: Skimpy Standards

#2: Presenting Poor Presence

#3: Permitting Pulling

#4: Dedicated to Desensitizing

#5: Tolerating Teeth

#6: Missing Management

#7: Misguided Methods

#8: Suspecting Sabotage

#9: Tenderness before Trust

#10: Shortsighted Selection

#1: Skimpy Standards

James attended our professionally guided, owner-trained service-dog class with his dog, Cazal. James served in the navy and had been deployed to Afghanistan twice before the age of twenty, being discharged when he developed posttraumatic stress disorder (PTSD). When I commented that his dog's name was quite unusual, he replied that it had been that of a buddy who had died on the battlefield next to him. Very sad.

James arrived at class with his mother and stepfather. His mother seemed a bit overprotective, while his stepdad suggested that idea of a service dog for the son was silly.

The exercise we were working on was "leave it." The words are a notice to the dog that he should shut down his attention on some sort of trigger, such as a cat or squirrel, a person on a skateboard, or the sound of kids playing in the distance. The process is simple. When a distraction is presented to a dog, he is told to "leave it." The cue is to be spoken quietly and calmly. The expectation is that the dog should stop focusing on the distraction and regain self-restraint. If the dog doesn't change his behavior when he hears the warning, he receives a collar correction. As you now know, this is based on the four steps to canine socialization.

Since controlling a cat or corralling a squirrel is challenging, we start this exercise with a distraction that is easy to manipulate and that most dogs find irresistible: hot dogs. Once the dog learns to ignore a tidbit of meat, we can present more advanced temptations. The standard is defined as, "dog may not sniff or snatch the food that falls at his feet, and he should discontinue excessive attention to it."

To learn whether the dog is actually interested in the hot dog, we begin by offering a small morsel. If he finds the treat delicious, we move on.

The handler asks the dog to sit. Since our standard for "sit" doesn't include "you may sniff or grab food," it is fair to correct the dog if he goes after the falling goodie while he is under the sit command. The instructor tosses the piece of hot dog at the dog's feet. The handler must pay attention. If the dog begins to move toward the treat, the person should calmly give the warning phrase, "Leave it." If the dog does not heed the warning and cease his movement toward the food, the handler delivers a correction. Then we repeat the process to make certain that the dog absorbed the lesson. On the second attempt, the handler should not have to deliver any physical correction, because the dog should have learned to obey the warning words and refrain from snatching the treat.

Very few novice handlers are successful on the first attempt; however, most are able to change their dog's behavior on the second or third try. It's important to understand that, at the time we present this new exercise, the dogs have already learned about receiving a correction when we taught the standards for sit, down, and heel. So, just about any dog can assimilate the expectation in a few repetitions.

The three other students there that day were able to teach their dogs to "leave it" without requiring a collar check after the initial correction, but James was struggling. Time and time again, he allowed Cazal to eat the food. Each time Cazal scarfed up a piece of hot dog, it became more difficult to teach him that he mustn't do so. For him, the hot dog was a reward associated with the cue words "leave it," so they didn't become a warning that he must refrain from doing so. After about six failed attempts, I decided to call for a break in the exercise to take a moment to think.

During the pause, James's mother approached me. "I don't think you understand that James has PTSD. He has a traumatic brain injury, so his brain has been altered. I don't think he has the physical capacity to give a correction as fast as you expect him to." It was an interesting defense. I wasn't sure how I felt about it, but her husband rolled his eyes. Clearly, he did not agree. I told her that I would take her concerns into consideration as I decided how to proceed.

For a number of reasons, including Cazal's safety and well-being, James had to be able to command his dog to "leave it." I recalled walking my own dogs through the alley behind my apartment in Chicago. It seemed that we always encountered a tasty danger like chicken bones scattered around a Dumpster. My dogs would have grabbed them up in an instant if I had not been able to direct them to ignore them. James was hoping to train Cazal to accompany him in public places as his service dog. Cazal could be enticed by any number of possible distractions; it was up to James to instruct him that his behavior was not acceptable. Cazal could not whine if he saw an object of affection. He could not bark at something that spooked him. He could not eat the cracker crumbs under a child's high chair at a restaurant. For all such situations, we recommend using the "leave it" warning.

Training does not end even once a person trains his dog to a very high standard. The dog will continue to encounter potential distractions. James had to learn how to communicate to Cazal when something was off-limits—not just at the beginning of their relationship, but for the rest of the dog's life. I needed to figure out a way to convey that to James.

When we reconvened the class, my husband and training partner, Robert, stepped up and offered to take over the lesson. I had noticed him eavesdropping when I'd talked with James's mother. I stepped back and let Robert address the class. He had served in the military for ten years; perhaps he had an instructional strategy that would be better suited for James.

In one hand, Robert held a bottle with bleach in it, and in the other, he had a piece of hot dog. He held up the piece of meat and sprayed it generously with the cleaner. Then, he held it out to the nearest person and asked her to take a sniff. "Does it smell like bleach?" he asked.

The woman's eyes widened as she nodded.

"Get ready, James," Robert said. Without pausing more than a couple of seconds, he tossed the treat right at Cazal's feet.

I heard a few gasps. Perhaps one was from my own lips. What was my husband thinking?

The real question was whether James would permit his dog to snatch up that poisoned morsel.

No. James did not let Cazal eat the bleach-soaked treat.

Robert bent over, picked up the piece of hot dog, and popped it into his own mouth, chewed, and swallowed. Then he pulled the tainted piece out of his pocket to illustrate that he had never put Cazal in danger. He had performed a sleight of hand. Of course, none of us, including James, had seen it.

Lydia's dog, Angel, spent a few weeks with us for training. When Lydia dropped her off, she listed the many things that Angel did that she "wanted fixed!" At the conclusion of the training, Lydia and her daughter arrived for the owner instruction. As we discussed the education that Angel had received, I described the necessity for setting standards so that everyone, including the dog, was aware of what behaviors were not acceptable. "It's the owner's job to decide what the standards are," I said. Is the dog permitted to bark out the window? Do you mind if she jumps up on people? Can she get on the furniture?"

"No!" Lydia and her daughter responded in stereo with great vehemence, interrupting my typical spiel.

"No, what?" I asked.

"No, she cannot get on the furniture. We fixed that right away!"

"So, you don't want her to get on the furniture?"

"No, we already fixed that. She has never been permitted on the furniture. I have a white couch. She cannot get up there. We fixed that when we first got her."

I found it interesting that Lydia's initial list of issues had been quite extensive. This typically means that the client has struggled to communicate any standards to the dog. Yet, it sounded as if Lydia had figured out how to prevent Angel from getting on her couch. "Do you have a baby gate at the living-room door?" I asked.

"No, but she's not allowed in the formal living room or the dining room. But she can go in the family room. She just can't get on the couch."

"How do you prevent her from going into the formal living room and dining room? Do you close the doors?" I asked.

"No, there are no doors. I can't put up gates, because my elderly mother lives with us, and she struggles if there are barriers."

"So, then, how did you teach Angel not to go in those rooms?"

"We just told her she couldn't," Lydia explained.

"What method did you use? How did you tell her what you wanted?" I questioned.

"I don't remember, exactly, but we just could not allow her to go in there, so we just worked on it."

"And, the couch? How did you teach her not to get up on the couch?"

"I'm not sure what we did, exactly. We just didn't let

her up there. I couldn't deal with dog hair on that five-thousand-dollar couch, you know?" she replied.

One of the most important elements in training a dog is being *serious* about it. Lydia couldn't even remember what she had done with Angel, but she knew that the dog was not going to get on the couch, and she had been serious about it. I suspect she had done some combination of interrupting Angel when she was about to get on the couch, like shouting or clapping her hands, paired with a physical consequence, like grabbing her and dragging her off the couch. It probably wasn't the slickest method, but it had worked. Angel understood that the couch was off-limits. The fact that Lydia was able to teach her dog to stay out of specific rooms and off certain furniture suggested to me that she probably didn't really need a professional to train her dog as much as she needed to take seriously the "fixing" of other aspects of the dog's behavior.

I believe that James was finally able to correct Cazal for going after the food because he ultimately took the situation seriously when he thought it was life threatening. This book is about the mistakes that dog owners make, and most commonly, the errors are due to the human's condition. A dog's bad behavior is not usually because the owners fail to execute a good method perfectly. Of course, I would rather that Angel had learned about boundaries with a clearer technique, but as long as the method that Lydia had used was effective and not abusive, I had to admit that it was successful. For that reason, I cannot completely fault it. After all, there is almost always more than one way to achieve a goal. However, if we are not committed to accomplishing the mission, we are not going to succeed. What I have come to know for certain is that one must take an endeavor seriously, or attainment is unlikely.

There is no point in coming up with standards if you are not sincere in upholding them. If you choose to commit, then establishing standards is critical. The four steps to canine socialization begin with setting standards. These define the behavior that you expect from your dog. This may include curbing jumping on people, tables, or counters. Eliminating verbal protests like whining or barking is an excellent standard to uphold. Preventing a dog from triggering on squirrels or kids on bikes may be on your list. Waiting before exiting a door is a valuable standard. Curtailing the licking of plates that are going into the dishwasher, sticking a nose in the refrigerator, and grabbing a piece of tissue out of a wastebasket are all good standards to set.

There are two zero-tolerance-policy standards that I believe must be established for all dogs. They are "no canine teeth on human flesh" and "no pulling." I discuss those in later sections of this chapter.

The point I make here is that before any sort of training method can be established with a dog, the owner must first define the standards for behavior. Quite often, this first step is never accomplished. Then, when the dog jumps up on your neighbor's child and knocks the kid over, you are in a losing position to address the unacceptable behavior. If you have considered that you do not want your dog to jump up, then you can pay attention to any signs that she is about to lose control and launch herself upward. At that point, you stand a much higher chance of successfully correcting your dog's behavior. I often recommend setting up training scenarios so that you are fully prepared to address a behavior when it happens.

If you intervene at the stage when your dog is

contemplating the naughty behavior, the intensity level of the correction can be lower and yet still be effective. You will also be acting proactively rather than reactively. It is nearly impossible for a dog to learn when the owner reacts after a behavior is presented rather than preemptively addressing it. Proactivity is a quality that defines good leaders.

Before anything happens—perhaps even before you acquire your dog—it is critical to establish the standards that you want to set for her behavior. Then you must contemplate your daily priority list and where you plan to uphold your dog's training among everything else that is going on in your life. How serious are you about your dog's daily education?

I knew a man who had smoked for fifty years. Then, his daughter had a little baby girl. When he held that innocent infant for the first time, his daughter said, "You know I love you, Dad. But you cannot hold my baby if you continue to smoke. You smell like an ashtray, and I don't want the baby to exist in that environment." The man quit smoking the following day and never had another cigarette. This represents the pinnacle of setting priorities.

Either you decide to be serious about upholding the behavior you set for your dog or you don't. It has less to do with the method you use than your commitment to maintain the standard. A mistake that dog owners make is to fail to seriously set standards for behavior. Only after that line in the sand has been drawn is there any reason to move forward with a specific technique to train your pup.

#2: Presenting Poor Presence

A quick Internet search yields a lot of information about why people quit their jobs. One of the most common is bad management. "People Leave Managers, Not Companies" is one article at Forbes.com. The *Harvard Business Review* has one starting with, "In general, people leave their jobs because they don't like their boss..."

I happen to think that dogs "quit" working for bad human leaders, too, regardless of the benefits package they receive—like top-quality food or daily belly rubs. For that reason, it's important to define what a good dog leader is. Before we evaluate the *actions* of a good leader, it's important to move a layer deeper: down to a person's *energy*. It is that intangible, unmeasurable quality that genuine leaders possess. It can be called *presence*.

When functioning at their best, leaders present calm confidence. They are comfortable in their own skins—meaning that they do not fear showing their authentic selves to others. They do not fret. They do not become agitated. They do not lose their cool. They are relaxed, poised, effective, and self-assured. They project an aura of authority without being domineering.

The best way to assess whether an individual has true presence is by evaluating his attractiveness. I do not mean physical beauty but the draw a person has on others who ultimately benefit from the relationship. Presence is an energy exuded from within that leads others to trust and follow. My years of existing with dogs have taught me that dogs perceive "it" in humans as well, if not better, than other humans do.

If you do nothing else around a frantic dog but become *truly* calm and centered, you can significantly affect his demeanor. I have experienced the phenomenon dozens of times.

Suzanne arrived to a workshop with her Springer Spaniel, Beau. He dragged her across the room. He triggered on a Yorkshire Terrier named York, bowed, and barked. Suzanne seemed to enjoy that he presented the bowing behavior, but her face scrunched up in anxiety at the bark; it was quite piercing. She took the opportunity to wrap his leash around her wrist and forearm because it was the first time there was a bit of slack available. As the door opened and Charlie the chocolate Labrador Retriever entered, pulling his owner, Beau mirrored Charlie's energy and raced toward him. Suzanne was dragged along like comet dust.

When class began, the students were asked to sit down; there were two chairs per eight-foot table, which should have offered plenty of room for each participant to keep his or her own dog close by. Still, Beau crawled toward York, whose owner picked him up, fearing for her little dog's life. It was obvious that Beau then triggered on the fear energy that York's owner had presented, because he uttered a new woof—one with some warning behind it. Suzanne pulled on Beau's leash and dragged him away from the Yorkie. Beau took the cue to travel 180 degrees in the opposite direction toward "Chevy the Heavy," a pudgy Bulldog. With each offense, Suzanne became more and more agitated and distressed by her dog's behavior.

Beau pressed Suzanne's buttons, and she responded. Her reactions tended to encourage Beau to present additional behavior that irritated her and sent her into a frenetic state of mind. Beau incessantly tried to climb into Suzanne's lap. She became tense and whined at him to stay down. Beau whined back and clawed at her legs. They were creating a huge snowball of hectic, hysterical activity that seemed to have no end. It was affecting everyone in the room.

When I called a break, Suzanne came to the front of the class—perhaps I should say that Beau dragged his owner there—and she asked if I could hold her dog's leash while she went to the restroom. Although the facilities were adequate to accommodate a person and her dog, I obliged.

I was sitting in a chair, not standing with authority. Yet, at the moment of the leash hand-off, Beau's behavior dramatically changed. Beau uncoiled. He tried to follow his owner as she walked off but met the end of his leash. Instead of attempting to pull me out of my chair, Beau returned to my side, sat, and then gently leaned on my leg. He released a deep breath. The tension in his muscles relaxed. Then, he did something that he had not done with Suzanne all morning. He looked up into my eyes with his ears back in a submissive position. His mouth relaxed, and he began to pant—not excessively, but as a way to release some of the pent-up heat from his earlier chaotic behavior.

The whole while, I had done nothing. In fact, I did not pay attention to Beau. I prepared myself to handle a serious jerk on the leash if he were to trigger on something; however, I withheld that information from Beau. I did not wrap the leash around my wrist or forearm. I did not project any sort of concern that Beau could flip me from my chair, grab York as he passed, or bark at Charlie. I was attentive but tranquil. I held the leash with the lightest touch possible while still remaining in sufficient physical contact to take charge of the dog if necessary.

The notion of being vigilant and relaxed at the same time is challenging for many. When some people are asked to be pay close attention to something, they can become tense and edgy. However, it is possible to be watchful and calm concurrently. Many professions require it—those of emergency medical technicians, hospital staff, people in the military, and even prison guards. The most common vocation where one must remain calm but attentive is parenting small children. It is an attribute you can practice and master. To be the best leader for a dog, honing that skill is imperative.

I did not speak to Beau. He didn't deserve such accolades. In fact, I held my head slightly up and turned away from him. It was the same way that I have seen my older dogs respond to crazy, young puppies that try to interact with them in disrespectful ways. Senior dogs do not always correct wayward puppies. Quite often, they intentionally disregard them. It's not all that different from human behavior. Overlooking someone is pretty powerful stuff—in humans and in dog society. It's a quick and noninvasive way to communicate the idea of status without working too hard. While they are always paying enough attention to take action if necessary, higher-ranking individuals often snub lower-ranking members of the pack. In the military, as a way of reinforcing this concept, the higher ranks do not eat in the same quarters as their reports.

Beau relaxed around me because I *knew* I was higher ranking than he was. I didn't have to tell him. I projected composed assurance because I was authentically composed and self-assured. I knew that I could control him; I didn't have to show him. That belief has to be real. As long as it is, then it works.

This is a talent that you can fake until you develop it. Consider the mother traveling with her two small children. She is on an unfamiliar route around a large city when she encounters a detour that takes her off the interstate. She comes to a stop in a neighborhood that is adorned with the paintings of gang members. Buildings are boarded up, and homes appear to be in ruins. She sees a group of young men whom she would refer to as hoodlums. She assumes they are doing a drug deal. She believes she sees a gun sticking out of one man's pocket. Just then, her five-year-old daughter exclaims, "Mommy, where are we?"

Using all the strength she can muster, in a firm but comforting tone, she replies, "We are on our way to Aunt Helen's house, just like I said." What she wanted to say might be, "I don't have a clue. I think we might all die. I can't see the next detour sign. Lord, help us all!" But she knows that if she does that, her daughter will cry, causing the three-year-old to erupt into a tantrum. When working with your dog, mustering the strength to appear more than you may feel you are can be invaluable at winning his trust in your leadership.

I remember telling one client who was a jumble of nerves that she should consider taking up meditation to achieve the tranquility that her dog needed. She called a few months later to say she had obtained professional help to resolve personal issues, and it had also improved her relationship with her dog. That's an extreme case, but it is testament that if the owner lacks some basic stability and serenity, the dog will mirror that lack of balance.

When I am working with a man who is struggling with his dog, I might inquire, "How much do you weigh?" OK, this is not a typical question (and—call me sexist—I don't ask this of any woman). Because it seems to come out of the blue, I often get a blank stare. I continue, "OK, you don't have to answer that. But you and I both know that you outweigh that dog by fifty or more pounds. Am I right?"

My point is to fuel the guy's fire about who is really the top dog. With males, I find that physical strength can be a potent motivator. If the man feels that the dog is controlling him, the dog will—regardless of its size. If he believes that he can control it, he will. That's the message. I'm not telling the guy to manhandle his dog. I'm telling him to change his attitude about who, in the relationship, he wants to be.

While I can sometimes push a client toward having better energy by reminding him or her that he or she is truly capable of controlling the dog, some people present a different challenge. It is not really about physical control at all (and most anyone should be able to handle a ten-pound pooch). It is about whether the owner actually aspires to the lead role in the relationship.

I have found that the most difficult clients to encourage toward leadership presence are those who are naturally nurturing. They often work in helping professions. It may be terribly uncomfortable for such a person to impose her will upon another, even a dog. The care and concern that they exude instinctively can be perceived as weakness by a dog. When you approach a dog with a sense of "Are you all right?" and, "Can I get you something to make you more comfortable?" it can be perceived as if you don't know what the dog needs. To a dog, that little blip of lack-of-take-charge can be unnerving and result in unruly behavior. If the dog doesn't sense that the person is confidently in control, regardless of the cause, there's a chance that it will attempt to take charge. Alternatively, it may simply ignore the person's intentions. Frequently, a dog will present with some level of turbulent energy when it feels leaderless.

A very common mistake that dog owners make is to mirror their dog's frantic energy rather than asking it to mirror their own calm, confidence. Of course, this is not intentional—it is just what occurs when the person is faced with a dog that is out of self-restraint. Learning to recognize when your dog is pushing your buttons is the first step, but the resolution happens when you present good energy and expect the dog to parrot your relaxed attitude.

10 Most Common Mistakes Dog Owners Make

While working on developing good presence, it is also important to eliminate "bad presence." My experience tells me that a large number of dog owners attempt to shame their dogs into behaving properly. Somewhere it must be written that one should use a specific tone of voice to control a dog. Because of this urban myth, many of my clients believe that they need to project an intimidating tenor in order for their dog to obey. I must remind them that dogs do not use verbal dialogue as a primary source of communication. That is a human thing to do. For that reason, using vocal nuances may not be the best strategy to help a dog understand your expectations.

On the topic of comparing species, it must be noted that dogs and humans are vastly different when it comes to acting "in charge." I have learned that the top dog is especially quiet. He rarely overreacts. He assumes a position from which he can view his world. He is often the dog lying on the top step of the porch or on top of a picnic table, back of the couch, or other surface where he can observe his domain.

He remains silent. The top dog doesn't bark incessantly. He rarely gets up from his lounging position to address minor events in the environment. He simply remains unruffled but attentive to his surroundings. If he sees a dog behaving in a way that is potentially disrespectful, he gives a little lip curl or a nearly inaudible growl. If the offending dog doesn't change course, then he quickly, without emotions or other residual baggage, physically corrects the wayward pup. There is an expectation that the lower-ranking ones pay sufficient attention to him that they witness his warnings. He is not going to waste energy reminding them repeatedly of their impending offense.

On the other hand, there are primates. A chimpanzee may grab a huge tree branch still adorned with half-drying leaves, and drag it across the ground. He moves laterally in front of those he is trying to impress. As he shakes the branch, the leaves rustle and enhance the effect he is striving to stage. He may give a holler or scream to make himself appear larger than life. A bouncer at a bar will puff up his chest, lift his chin, straighten his shoulders, and walk directly into the personal space of the individual he is trying to intimidate into leaving the establishment. A parent may begin with a normal tone of voice when commanding her child, "Go brush your teeth." But if the kid doesn't obey, it's not uncommon for him or her to speak louder and harsher. "I said, *go brush your teeth*!" We humans struggle to remain calm in tone when we feel that our subject is defying our authority. Dogs simply go right to the consequence. No nagging. No anger. No frustration. No tone of voice.

It is as if a dog is saying through his actions, "I don't hate you. I'm not upset. I am not frustrated or disappointed. My ego is not bruised. I just don't want you to climb on my back." They warn calmly and then correct effectively. No emotions. So refreshing. I wish it were the human approach. We tend to feel a need to escalate our voices and move to shaming tones and phrases like, "What is wrong with you?"

Shame is not the same as guilt. Guilt is a definition of culpability. The dog can be guilty of shredding the pillow, but he doesn't understand that he did something wrong, even if you enunciate every word as if it had an extra four vowels in each syllable. "*Whaaaat diiiiid yooooou doooo? Baaaaaad dog!*"

It is hard to use shaming tones without projecting disappointment energy. I am certain that dogs feel that shift. They recognize that we are not pleased or that we are enraged. In response, they submit. They put their ears back. They drop their heads. They slither across the ground, trying to either escape their owner's wrath or to make up by groveling at his or her feet. The uninformed owner believes that the signs of submission must imply that the dog knew that he shouldn't have chewed up the new pillows. Nothing could be further from the truth—and to believe so is wholly unfair to the dog.

The other "tone of voice" that is often implemented by errant owners is the domineering pitch. Many clients have told me that another member of their family has better control over the dog because he or she uses his or her tone of voice more effectively. What is probably happening is that the more successful individual is using intimidating tones with the dog. This is often a male. Men, in general, have more testosterone in their system than do women. Dogs understand the use of testosterone for intimidation. I see it when intact males are around females in estrus. There's a lot of posturing that goes on between the boys.

However, on a day-to-day basis, I do not believe that dogs use sex hormones to control each other. I say that because it is often a female dog that is in charge of other dogs in the house, and many dogs are spayed or neutered anyway. It's not uncommon for a four-pound female Chihuahua to dominate a ninety-pound male German Shepherd Dog. The four-step process to canine socialization does not necessitate extreme power or force. So, female dogs (and humans) can be as successful at ruling the roost as males.

Nonetheless, male humans are known for projecting the vibe of, "If you don't do that, I will kill you," and while they may not really mean it, they know that they could if they wanted to. That energy typically causes a dog to present submissive behaviors. The dog doesn't know why his person is so upset, but he submits simply out of respect for authority and to remain in the pack. He feels the threat that is underneath the intimidating tones.

To clarify my point, I ask you to consider this scenario. You travel to another country where they do not speak your language. Your host goes to work, and you stay home waiting for his return. During that time, you get a Coke out of the fridge, you watch television while sitting on the couch, you use the restroom once, you eat a cookie from a plate on the counter, and you take a book from the shelf and sit in the recliner by the window and read a bit. When your friend returns from the office, he walks in the door, looks around, and then raises his voice at you in shaming or domineering tones. He flails his arms about or shakes a finger in your face. Maybe he snaps his finger at you and points. You know two words of the foreign language he is speaking—your name and the word "bad." You hear him pair up your name with "bad" a few times while he scowls at you, stomps his feet, and leaves the room with a "Humph!"

Because dogs are naturally acquiescent to humans, partly because they have been domesticated and partly because they are a social species that recognizes hierarchy, they respond to a higher-ranking one's displeasure by showing submission. This doesn't mean that the dog knows what he did wrong. In fact, he may not be guilty of any behavior (sometimes the owner is wrong about what happened in her absence). By presenting submissive gestures, the dog is attempting to say, "Hey, I know you are not pleased right now. I just want you to know that I still honor your position, I still respect you as the leader, and I have no intention of usurping your authority." That's what I think.

If you were unable to determine if your friend was not happy with you because you ate a cookie, had a Coke, sat in his chair, or forgot to put the toilet seat down, a dog isn't going to know that chewing up the pillows a few hours before you arrived home has upset you.

A dog cannot learn and adapt to "better" behavior

through a shift in its owner's tone of voice. Dogs don't use tone of voice to set boundaries for behavior. The quietest dog is the top dog. He doesn't babble on and on, escalating his displeasure by whining, nagging, dominating, or shaming the offender. He just cuts straight to the consequence and delivers it before anything can escalate. That way, the correction doesn't have to be very severe. The offender is still in the state of intention—not yet performing the naughty deed—when the correction is delivered. Wouldn't it be nice if we humans could learn to emulate the ways of our pet dogs?

A common mistake dog owners make is believing that using a shaming or domineering tone of voice will change the dog's behavior. Presence is as much a state of mind as it is an activity. Projecting an aura of authority with poise and relaxed assurance is a more successful way to develop a trusting relationship with your dog.

#3: Permitting Pulling

A few years ago, I was contacted by a company that organized pet expositions around the country. They held events in many large cities, including Saint Louis, which is about an hour from my home. At the time, I was a certified pet first-aid and CPR instructor. I was asked to provide one twenty-minute demonstration, and in exchange, I was offered a free booth space. I thought it was a very good trade and agreed to participate.

The expo was staged in a large convention center, and participants were invited to bring their pets to the venue. This was not a dog-specific event. In attendance with their owners were parrots perched upon shoulders, ferrets on harnesses, and cats in baby strollers. Of course, the species that outnumbered all others was dog. Since our space had been provided free of charge, I figured we would be tucked away in a corner, away from the action. But that was not the case. Our booth was down a main artery, not far from the entrance. I was able to observe thousands of people over the course of the day. The expo organizers later noted that nearly three thousand attended with a canine in tow.

There were dogs wearing buckle collars, martingale collars, choke collars, prong collars, head halters, harnesses of all varieties, even dogs donning multiple devices of control and restraint. One woman was steering her dog from behind. It had a halter on its face that came around its left side and a body harness attached to a leash at its right. The owner held one leash per hand as if driving a plow horse. It was outrageous. Several folks had small dogs in body slings much like those used to carry babies. I also saw dogs that wore one or more electronic devices around their necks.

It was obvious that people had a variety of opinions regarding how to tether themselves to and control their dogs. However, in that congregation of three thousand, I saw just two dogs that were walking calmly on loose leads under self-restraint. One was a little black Cocker Spaniel, and the other was a beautiful Belgian Tervuren. Every other dog that I saw that day had tension on its neck and was pulling its owner. Even if I only saw half of the dogs that were there, that's far less than 1 percent that were not pulling their owners. Shocking.

While having the right presence with your dog is the most important attitudinal characteristic to develop, preventing pulling on the leash is the most important physical skill to cultivate as a dog owner. You might find this claim hard to believe if you examine just about any image of pet dogs and their people. Nearly every image in magazines, on TV, and on the Internet shows a dog walking out in front of its person and the leash in direct tension with the dog's neck. Travel to a city park or just around your neighborhood, and look at the folks walking their dogs on tight leashes. The dog is out in front of the human. Even if you attend a dog-agility event, where dogs are supposed to be trained, you will see most of the canines straining on their leads with stress on their necks. For those who don't want their dogs to experience neck strain, the dogs are on a harness. But, still they are pulling out ahead of their owner.

There are many reasons that a dog should not be permitted to pull on the leash. None is more important than to eliminate the chance for physical harm. Constant pressure on the dog's neck can cause damage to the trachea. Many dogs do not get the pleasure of going into public places because their owners are afraid of the damage that may be associated with the pressure of the collar. The constant gagging sound is too much to bear.

Holding the leash of a dog that pulls is also potentially damaging for the human owner. Many of my clients have shared stories about dislocated shoulders, torn ligaments, or even a broken kneecap as a result of a dog that pulls on the leash. Clearly, permitting a dog to yank on the lead must be discouraged simply to reduce injury to dogs and their people.

From a relationship and behavioral perspective, pulling is a testament of disrespect. A dog that is pulling is leading, not following. If we want to resolve the issue, we must again explore the relationship between the dog and his owner.

Based on what I have heard from hundreds of my clients, I would say that the primary reason they are not willing to stop the pulling behavior is that they do not want to hurt their dogs by delivering a correction. If you are of a similar mind-set, I simply ask you: is a moment of discomfort worth eliminating a life of physical and psychological abuse? Yes, I am going to go there. A dog that must exist with constant restraint around its neck is experiencing discomfort that could be considered abusive.

I equate the quandary that people have regarding correcting their pulling dog to giving a child a vaccination. Yes, needles cause pain, but we must weigh that moment of discomfort versus the child getting a deadly or debilitating disease. For a dog, is it not worth a moment of pain for a lifetime of freedom from constant strain around the neck? Subjecting a dog to unrelenting tension on his neck is unacceptable, especially since pulling behavior can be curbed using the appropriate method.

I have lived with a pack of dogs for nearly thirty

years. Observing them has truly helped me understand dog social order. Many of my dogs have been Border Collies. They tend to display a strong expectation for social etiquette in the group. They are, after all, incredible control freaks. It would be challenging for a little dog to pilot a flock of sheep that collectively weighs thousands of pounds more if it was not equipped with a strong desire to contain and control.

From observing my pack, I have come to know many things about dog decorum. For example, when I take a group of my dogs on a run alongside my ATV, there is a rule (which I did not impose) that no lower-ranking dog can pass the vehicle. When an inexperienced pup tries to outrun it, a more senior dog will outflank it and turn it back. This is herding behavior displaced onto another dog rather than livestock. But this is not about "contain and control" as much as it is about deference. I know that my dogs recognize me as the higher-ranking one, so when an older dog sees a younger one disrespecting that relationship, it takes notice and addresses the wayward pup.

I have seen a few examples of first-rate dog professionals who can walk a large group of dogs; none of which crosses the path of the human's knees even when they are off lead. The dogs' obvious self-restraint is not a result of being micromanaged or under constant verbal control. In my experience, this behavior is also not an outcome of teaching the dogs about a specific line they may not cross. It is rooted in a general understanding of follower versus leader. It is an attribute that lives inside each dog, but it only comes out when the rapport between dog and human is properly established. Pulling on lead isn't about a physical position. It is about a state of mind. At its source is the need to respect an authority figure.

Because pulling on the lead is not about a specific

location relative to the owner, any technique that attempts to resolve pulling behavior by rewarding the dog for remaining in a particular position will not successfully solve the problem. Pulling cannot be resolved by teaching the dog where you want him to remain. It is rectified when you tap into his natural; social-species need to follow a leader. Pulling is resolved when the dog learns where he must *not* go rather than where he should be.

Before they experience that lesson, scent-motivated dogs typically have their noses on the ground, following a trail of pleasure. When they are snout to the ground, it is as if they are reading a newspaper, gathering all of the intelligence about the neighborhood. Vision-motivated dogs will have their heads up, scanning for possible threats or objects that may be enjoyable to engage with, like...*squirrels*! These dogs are not aware that their person would prefer that they do not pull on the leash during the entire walk about the park. They can endure a lot of jerking and tugging and simply get back on task to accomplish their own agendas. They stay focused on their objectives regardless of the discomfort their owners are attempting to impart on them.

As I came to see in grand scale at the pet expo, there is no magical tool that will stop a dog from pulling. I saw hundreds of dogs pulling on every type of collar, halter, and harness, including the equipment that I typically use to deliver highly effective corrections. Many of the tools do what they were designed to do, as long as you employ them right. But any of them will fail if you do not use them properly. Proper usage requires the handler to have the right attitude and motivation to resolve the issue.

What some people do not fully recognize is that if leash-pulling behavior is resolved, many other issues cease as well. My husband, Robert, who is a great dog trainer in his own right, believes that with many dogs, dog owners completely forget that they are dog owners all the time, not just when they are training the dog, practicing what they have learned, or addressing a behavior issue. Their presence dissolves away.

When I state that a dog owner must be in control of his or her dog at all times, I am often asked, "When does my dog get to be a dog?"

Consider a mother who is preparing dinner as her three kids are in the backyard, playing. At times, she can see them through the window, but the yard is larger than her view. Still, she can hear them. They are not "on command" when they are playing, but they are still her kids. If she hears their voices escalate to the point where she thinks there might be a fight or perhaps cursing, she opens the door and reminds them that yelling isn't allowed. She expects them to oblige. They are to remain social even though they are not on a direct command.

When she calls them in for dinner, she tells them to wash their hands and set the table. At that point, they are "under command," so to speak. After that, they must stay indoors, but they are not under any "direct orders" until the meal is served. At the table, they are expected to stay seated and must chew with their mouths shut. These are general social expectations.

You can see that the role of the parent never wanes. The kids are expected to behave to a general social standard all the time, and if they begin to move outside those boundaries, the parent warns them to regain their self-restraint. At times, they are asked to perform specific tasks and are expected to complete them to the standards that were set. And so it is with dog ownership. The dog does not have to be under a direct command all the time; however, she must be socially compliant. This means that barking at squirrels out the window is not acceptable, just like kids' screaming is not tolerated. Such indiscretions must be addressed by someone of higher rank; then the kids (or dog) can go back to playing within the general limits of good behavior.

Pulling on the leash is like hitting your sister. It is never acceptable. I believe that one of the main reasons people permit their dogs to pull on the leash is that they simply don't recognize that the dog is doing so. Step two of the fundamental canine socialization formula is: *pay attention*. A dog needs feedback immediately, or he may revert to his old habits and assume that pulling is acceptable. Receiving an over-the-top, intensely harsh correction paired with angry energy three minutes into the walk is unfair—and unsuccessful at resolving the problem. The idea of being present in the moment disappears, however, as the person contemplates picking up the kid at school, buying something for dinner, or getting to an appointment.

Again, this zero-tolerance standard of no pulling is the most important physical skill that a dog owner must learn and present to his dog to establish the proper leader-follower relationship. Teaching the dog the standard is not nearly as difficult as paying sufficient attention to a dog's behavior when he is on leash and addressing the problem in the very early stages of intention. That is the fair way to correct a dog.

I avoid a significant challenge of puppyhood because I do not put a collar or leash on a puppy until I'm ready to teach it how to behave on a leash. That is when it is around seven months old. I know that not everyone lives in an environment that can accommodate this sort of early education. However, if I can prevent a young pup from developing a tolerance of pulling on the leash, I can teach it about loose-lead etiquette in an hour when the time is right. That is my preference.

I have a fenced yard. I have older dogs. I allow my socially balanced older dogs to educate a puppy I am raising through the sort of play that it should experience. Wolves do not take their pups on hunts. I don't take young pups on walks. I do not want to give collar corrections to a young dog. I prefer to use my hands to give a quick jab to a pup that jumps on me or tries to put its teeth on me. Otherwise, I adhere to strong management and avoid allowing bad habits to form. Then, when the adolescent dog is ready to receive leash training, I have a clean slate for a student that is psychologically old enough and ready to learn. That is my recommendation.

There are sports and duties that may require pulling. Skijoring, carting, service-dog tasks like wheelchair assistance or guiding for the sight impaired are a few examples. Those behaviors are trained and in my opinion should not be implemented until a dog has been appropriately socialized, including with a no-pulling policy. Trained tasks that include pulling are typically associated with specific equipment that will not harm the dog when he pulls its weight or that of his human partner. I do not recommend a dog to be asked to pull against a collar that is around his neck for any sport or work. When the leash is attached to the collar, the dog must not pull.

Finally, the huge windfall of establishing and then

maintaining a no-pulling rule is that the dog can be off leash and recognize the owner as the leader. This is opposed to considering the owner as the one who constantly restrains him. Restraint can result in an impulse for freedom (a.k.a. running off). A dog that is not subjected to constant tension but taught to hang out under the umbrella of his owner's authority is likely to remain close by once the leash is removed.

Teaching a dog that pulling is not acceptable commonly results in successful off-lead management. However, some breeds have been developed with an intense drive to do work, which can override their need to stick around with their humans. Hounds are designed to follow the trail of game, and the expectation is that the hound's owner must keep pace with the dog if he wants to secure the quarry. Breeds with that sort of disposition must be taught the no-pull policy while on leash. Unfortunately, they may not stick around while off leash, so proper management is required.

To be very frank, I think that many people enjoy the security that the leash offers. The possibility of failure when the leash is removed sends many people to the dark recesses of anxiety and fear that they simply cannot endure. It is sad for the dog and the owner alike, but a need to "feel" the dog's presence pulling at the end of the leash can be the reason that some owners allow it to continue.

Permitting a dog to pull on the leash is an all-too-common mistake that dog owners make. Resolving it may remove several of the next mistakes from the list; however, I still recommend that you read on!

#4: Dedicated to Desensitizing

There is a dog-training strategy referred to as desensitizing. It is typically described as a method for reducing fear but also to lessen aggression or overly assertive behavior. Some folks have suggested that it can diminish extreme excitability as well. Since fight, flight, and excessive exuberance are three types of antisocial behavior, desensitizing is said to help socialize a dog—so let's evaluate it against the four steps of socialization.

Sean brought us his young female Standard Poodle for early training. While he didn't say so at first, he wanted to train Juliet as a service dog, as he suffers from Parkinson's disease. At five months old, Juliet received three weeks of basic training, and then Sean and his wife got five hours of handler instruction where they learned philosophy and practical techniques.

A little later on, Sean said that he wanted Juliet to act as his service dog on an airline trip in about eight months. We talked about what to expect at airport security. He said that he intended to visit a friend's small, prop plane to desensitize Juliet to the sound of it as a way to prepare for the trip on a larger jet.

Since Juliet had been through a comprehensive training regimen with us, she had been exposed to some experiences that could trigger fear, aggression, or overly excited behavior. The point, however, was not to desensitize her to any *specific* condition. It would be impossible to train a dog to be well mannered in the real world if we had to account for every possible trigger. After all, a client and his dog could encounter an elephant, a team of Clydesdale horses and wagon, or a hot-air balloon, and we do not have those available as training aids.

I informed Sean that he did not have to train Juliet specifically to the plane, but it could be a very good experience for him. If she did move out of self-restraint, he could reinforce the most important lesson she had already learned: to respect and obey her leader because he had shown that she could trust him to keep her safe under his command. This is the essence of proper dog socialization. As I've mentioned, most people struggle to maintain a dog's social compliance more than to train it to perform tasks. I suspect that desensitizing is really about helping a dog behave better around events and objects that trigger it to move out of social boundaries.

For example, it isn't mannerly to attack the vacuum cleaner. One acclimation strategy is to leave it in the middle of the room and periodically place a piece of cheese on it. As the dog gets familiar with the vacuum and gains the courage to snatch the morsel of cheese, encountering the vacuum becomes a "happy" event. However, I don't want my dog to think of a vacuum cleaner as a goodie-vending machine. I simply want my dog to ignore it when I use it.

The problem with the concept of desensitizing is that it puts all the power in the relationship between the dog and the trigger. The role of the human is to offer up the source of fear so that the dog can become familiar with the object or event. There is no leadership required. The dog is not asked to look up the chain of command and say, "Hey, I'm feeling uncomfortable in this situation. How should I behave?" The human is not responsible to teach the dog about what is unacceptable behavior. The focus is on the uncontrollable entity—the thing that generates the dog's misbehavior. We cannot regulate whether there are squirrels, birds, horses, cats, doorbells, men in hats, kids on bikes, trains, brooms, people using walkers, screaming children, jackhammers, balloons, or elephants in the world.

But we can control ourselves. That's actually the primary prerequisite of leadership. And, we can control our dogs to the extent that we acknowledge dogs are social animals that have been domesticated and are capable of integrating into our world with training and continued management. The power lies in the relationship between the human and the dog. Once the human initiates the four steps of socialization with the dog, the dog will accept that the human knows its language and will recognize the person as the higher-ranking one in the relationship.

This is not a bad thing: nature has very few flat organizational charts. The domestication process has stripped most dogs of the capacity to dominate a pack or to make important survival decisions for the group. Dogs are like children under two years old. They need a parent to call the shots for their physical and emotional well-being. When a person assumes ownership of a dog, she also must assume responsibility as its higher-ranking leader.

When I explained to Sean that he didn't need to desensitize Juliet to the sound of a plane engine, it didn't mean I thought it wasn't valuable for them to experience many different potentially challenging environments together. But the intention was not to desensitize Juliet to the sound, scent, sight, taste, or feeling of the possible triggers; it was to give her an opportunity to move from social (obedient) to antisocial (disobedient) behavior and Sean a chance to remind her that he establishes the boundaries for her behavior using the four-step process they had practiced hundreds of times.

Juliet could still fear the sound of the engine. She could still be excitable around little kids or act overly domineering around other dogs. We cannot control whether a dog is fearful, excitable, or overly assertive in any situation. We can only remind the dog that we expect a specific behavior and that if she begins to move toward breaking the boundary of that standard, we will give her a warning. If she doesn't heed the warning, we will give her a correction. The dog is left with the free will to determine her fate.

Let's be clear about a few things. First, during training, it *is* important to present events that can trigger all of the dog's senses—sight, sound, taste, smell, and touch. We also must recognize that dogs trigger on emotional experiences. The four-step socialization process should be explored by exposing the dog to all six of these possible triggers. Very specifically, the dog should be asked to perform a behavior he understands, like "sit and remain sitting." Then, he should be presented with distractions.

For *sight*, while the dog sits on command, a cat could enter the room. If the dog chooses to break his obedience to the sit command to visit the cat, then he is corrected. He should heed the warning and remain in the sitting position (in a calm, self-restrained manner).

Sound and *scent* distractions should be implemented in a similar manner.

For *touch*, as the dog sits on command, a plush toy is dropped to intentionally touch the dog. (This should be done lightly enough to avoid injury, of course.) The dog must not trigger from the touch and get out of the sit position.

For *emotion* distraction, while the dog sits on command, someone speaks in loving tones or a squeaky voice to the dog. (Do not use the dog's name or any known command words.) The dog should not trigger on the sweet nothings and get out of the sit. This is probably the hardest trigger to overcome for many dogs, mostly because owners may be completely unprepared to correct a dog that is responding to affection. Sadly, we must dedicate time to train service dogs to refrain from breaking a standard when it experiences a person speaking sweetly, because total strangers are likely to do just that to a dog that is wearing a service-dog vest in public, even if there are notices on it stating that the dog is working!

During a dog's socialization, the handler can expose it to as many different potential triggers across the six senses as desired. With each new experience, the dog learns more about the standard of obedience to a command like sit, heel, or down. Again, these events are not designed to desensitize the dog to the specific triggers. They are irrelevant, except that those that actually cause the dog to break obedience are more valuable as teachable moments.

However, years after the initial training to sit on command, no matter what, your dog could encounter an event or object that causes her to break obedience. But by that time, you will have had thousands of teachable moments, and you may simply need to give a calmly spoken warning word to help your dog regain self-restraint. Or, it may be the Goodyear Blimp of all triggers, and you may have to give a serious correction because your dog doesn't heed your warning word. Regardless, the dog will have a very clear understanding of why you gave her the correction; therefore it will be fair and just.

Thunderstorms can be especially traumatic to some dogs. We can attempt to desensitize a dog to storms by playing recordings of them, but I have not found that method to be successful. In Border Collies, fear of storms is a fairly common problem, so I have dealt with it often. Most of my dogs were less concerned with the actual sound than with shifts in barometric pressure that they could feel sometimes hours beforehand. That's why audio desensitizing isn't terribly useful. My dog Breeze used to attempt to run away during storms, chewing off doorknobs and ripping through screen doors. I never understood why he wanted to leave what I considered the safety of our house. But if I put Breeze in his crate before a storm, he remained calm. Kael, on the other hand, who had the same motivation to run, would chew the bars of a crate to the point of injuring himself. If he could lie by my side, he could weather the storm, so, that's how I managed him through his fears.

What is critical to understand is that we cannot fix fear; we can only address behavior. One of my clients said that her dog would get into the bathtub during storms and would sit, shaking and drooling. I responded, "What a smart dog. Isn't that the sort of place we are told to go during severe storms?"

"But she is shaking and drooling," the client replied.

"Well, if my dog were to drool, I would be grateful that she was in the tub, where I could just wash it down the drain."

"You don't understand. She is afraid!"

"We cannot fix that; I'm sorry to tell you. Is there a reason you don't like that your dog is in the tub during storms?"

"She is afraid, and I don't want her to be afraid."

"I've already said that we can't fix fear. Is there something else you would like your dog to do instead of drooling in the tub?"

If a client had told me that the dog shredded the window blinds during storms, well, then we would need to fix that. If the dog tried to climb up the owner's body and claw at her legs, we would need to fix that. If the dog barked incessantly or paced in front of the TV while we were trying to watch *Dancing with the Stars*, then we would need to fix that. We can fix behavior.

It is the fairest to teach a dog to perform a sit or

place them on an artificial scale of severity. The standard also includes when a dog grabs for a toy that the owner is picking up to throw during a game of fetch: no teeth.

The standard must start at six weeks old. Since puppies shouldn't leave the breeder's home until eight weeks or after, this means you need to communicate with the breeder to ascertain that she understands the importance of teaching wee, baby pups that they may not put their teeth on people. The standard includes disallowing any "teething" behavior by baby puppies. And, we can add that clothing is synonymous to skin, so the standard includes, "No teeth on human clothing, including shoelaces."

Just like pulling on the leash, this common problem is the result of the mistake of failure to establish a clear standard. When I explain that a dog should never put his teeth on a person at any time, many of my clients are somewhat surprised. There seems to be a desire to make the distinction between dogs that bite because they are aggressive and dogs that just are too ignorant to know better than to put their teeth on people. Sure, we can make that distinction, but does it really matter?

It is important to view this from the dog's perspective. We need to recognize the ambiguity that exists when we allow a puppy to chew on our hand or pull on our shoelaces. That vagueness leaves a pup believing that a human is of equal rank—like a littermate rather than a parent or higher-ranking dog in the family.

Let's go back to Lexie weaning her puppies. Puppies do not have teeth when they are born. That's a good thing for mama dogs. As their teeth emerge and they concurrently begin to get stronger at sucking, it becomes painful for the mother. I suspect that this provides the impetus for her to establish a weaning schedule. Baby teeth are sharp, and they hurt.

Besides helping to motivate the mother to wean her puppies, there is a secondary reason for ultra-sharp teeth. Between weeks three and four, puppies begin to recognize others, including a human who offers solid foods and their siblings. As they start to engage with their sisters and brothers, they use their most developed skill to explore. They have been using their mouths since the day they were born, so it is only reasonable to expect puppies to investigate their world and the others they encounter with their teeth. There is no ill will or malice directed toward the objects and individuals they bite, but that doesn't mean it doesn't hurt.

Siblings respond to the pain by yelping, pulling back, or biting back. Through that exchange, puppies begin to learn that they have an effect on other animals. Weaning is probably more emotional because it means the end of an important era in their lives. However, the painful snap from an irritated brother is probably more severe, and it often causes tantrums that sound like the cute and cuddly canines have morphed into little Tasmanian devils. The idea of bite inhibition has been related to the early learning that puppies acquire from playing with each other using their teeth and discovering how to regulate themselves.

As adolescents, which I consider to be between around six and eighteen months, puppies frequently play rough with other dogs in their pack. This play often includes mouthing behavior that can be so extreme that after a good romp, at least one of the dogs appears wet and foamy. Mouth wrestling, as it is sometimes called, is a common interaction between dogs of similar rank. But it is rare for a dog that considers himself high ranking to engage in such frivolity.

Younger dogs often present a submissive greeting: the pup attempts to nibble at an older dog's chin. It looks similar to what wolf puppies do to stimulate their parents to regurgitate food after a hunt. Typically, the older dogs simply lift their heads and walk away. On occasion, if a pup is very insistent, the higher-ranking dog will scold it with a growl and a snap. Besides that subordination behavior, younger dogs usually refrain from playing mouthing games with their elders. I believe that is because the elders prohibit it as a means of establishing and maintaining pack order and hierarchy.

For this reason, I recommend that physical interactions with dogs are appropriately measured. This is going to be a hard pill to swallow for people who enjoy wrestling with their dogs or what I refer to as "slapping the dog around." Slapping the dog is a sad but all-too-common phenomenon. While young men are the most likely to enjoy such games, I see all sorts of people engage in the behavior. These folks do not appreciate my term *slapping*, but that is exactly what they are doing. Using an open hand, they pat the dog, typically on the sides of the body, with a fairly powerful blow. They often use both hands—one hand slapping one side of the dog, then the other repeating the slaps on the other side. One can hear the *thud, thud, thud* of these smacks. It appears that some actually hit the dog hard enough that it loses balance and must right itself, which they consider a game. I have seen people perform this act with dogs as small as a four-pound Yorkie (of course, the slap is less intense than what folks might do to a Labrador Retriever, but pound for pound, it's sometimes more intense on the smaller dogs).

Slapping is often paired with grabbing. People grab the dog's fur or skin around the neck and tussle with it, waving the dog's head back and forth. This is usually accompanied with some sort of verbalization that incites the dog to become agitated or at least retaliatory.

It is also quite common to see people engage in teasing their dogs. Of course, these people refute such claims. But stepping briskly in front of (or actually deliberately on) a dog's toes to rile it into a state of excessive exuberance is not good game play. It is teasing. Side slapping, grabbing, and teasing are sometimes just part of a complete repertoire that a dog owner considers acceptable and even enjoyable interaction. Even belly rubs can be seriously over the top and seem to offer more enjoyment for the owner than the dog.

Yes, some dogs are excited by such interactions; however, excitement is not synonymous with happiness. A dog is happiest when it knows its position in the family and can trust a respected leader. Excitement can lead to jumping and nipping behavior. Of course dogs love to play, and some dogs like to mouth wrestle with other dogs. However, you do your dog a grand disservice by leaving it to question who is in charge and with whom it can brawl.

Taking on responsibility for someone, whether a worker, child, student, or dog, means that you may not be able to interact with that individual in certain ways and still be the best boss, parent, teacher, or dog owner. Playing games that are shared between equal-ranked dogs will leave your dog believing that you are equally ranked. Equally ranked dogs sometimes bite each other. It is unfair to leave your dog wondering if you permit biting or not.

This whole topic is probably making a number of readers squirm, because they simply do not want to acknowledge the idea that dogs are happiest in a hierarchy where they know their position. Those folks prefer to ignore the idea of pack dynamics and ranked social structure. A big part of science includes observation. Anyone who spends time with a group of socially balanced dogs will learn these fairly simple realities about our canine companions.

A common mistake that dog owners make, then, is to behave toward a dog as if they are equally ranked dogs that slap, grab, and tease. It is a very ambiguous message and makes it terribly difficult for the dog to concurrently recognize the owner's desire for obedience and respect. To uphold the standard of "no canine teeth on human flesh," we may not engage the dog in such a way that he believes it is acceptable or necessary to mouth, nip, or bite us.

If you are someone who enjoys a good wrestling match, you need to find another human who wants the same from you. You must terminate such conduct with your dog if you want to be a fair and benevolent leader. This does not mean you may not continue to lavish your dog with affection. But a kind stroke is not the same as a hard pat or a slap. As the higher-ranking one, you may enter your dog's personal space as you please. But do so in a respectful way, and your dog will return the deed.

There are dozens of fun, interactive games you may play with a dog without being heavy-handed. If you antagonize your dog into acting aggressively, you will create an antagonist. People with toy dogs often exclude themselves from such recommendations because they do not believe a toy dog can do significant damage. It is equally unacceptable to pester toy dogs into presenting violent behavior, especially while it is being held by the owner. Although some people find it funny, I consider it abusive.

I am always surprised when I have this conversation with clients who do not realize how cruel they have been acting toward their dogs. Legally, a snap, nip, or bite is the same thing if it causes damage. Yet, even more important to understand is that our dogs trust us. If we incite our dogs to put their teeth on us during an act we refer to as "play," it is terribly unfair to scold them for crossing our arbitrary line for naughty behavior. Most dogs offer us trust freely. To crush that trust because we mishandle them is simply unacceptable.

#6: Missing Management

"My dog is chasing cars," the man on the phone proclaimed.

"What is he doing on the road?" I asked.

Long pause.

"He's chasing cars," he replied with an edge in his voice, perhaps irritated that I might not have heard him the first time.

"Yes, I understand that. But what is he doing on the road?" I repeated.

The distinction I'm making here is that a dog that isn't permitted on the road cannot chase cars. We can either continue to allow the dog onto the road and conjure a bunch of solutions that may or may not work to eradicate the car-chasing behavior or properly manage the dog so that he doesn't have access to the road.

I think this man would have preferred to consider a host of possible options—things like tossing firecrackers at the dog or chucking a bucket of water at it out of a moving vehicle—rather than implement an actual management solution so that his dog wouldn't be killed.

When I moved to my current, rural location, I encountered a bit of culture shock regarding how folks consider dog ownership. Many of them believe that if they live in the country, their dogs can run loose. Anything less seemed like cruelty to them. It is difficult, if not impossible, to change an attitude about what a person believes is the right and noble thing to offer a dog—extreme freedom—because, well, "We live in the country."

I suspect some people believe that dogs should be granted extreme freedom because they would like the same. However, I argue that while vacations where we don't need clocks, sleep late, and party all night can be satisfying, we soon tire of such lack of structure. We ache to come home to a predictable routine. Dogs prefer structure too—perhaps even more than many humans. They are also incapable of assessing many of the dangers that exist in our human world, like traffic, deer hunters in the woods, or chicken bones in the alley. If you choose to own a dog, you must constantly consider its environment. Good dog management involves either controlling the environment or the dog within it.

Thinking that I was going to hear the same old argument about how dogs should run loose, I listened not so patiently to a potential client:

"I need your help. Molly ran over to the neighbor's house again and chased their cat. This time, they called the police. I have to do something."

I replied, "Well, clearly you need to either fully supervise her when she is outdoors or keep her confined to a fenced area when she is outside alone."

"Oh, we have a fenced yard. She doesn't get out of there."

"How is she getting to the neighbor's house?" I asked.

"Out the front door," replied the owner.

I envisioned careless children who let Molly slip by them when they opened the door. "Well, you will have to take control of Molly when you open the door so she can't race out," I explained.

"She doesn't do it when we are by the door. The knob isn't real good, so she can just push her way out when she wants," the woman said.

"I would be happy to train your dog, but it sounds like you just need a seven-dollar latch from True Value," I concluded.

Potty accidents in the house are also often due to a lack of good management. One woman told me, "Gordon is going downstairs to pee behind the water heater. Otherwise, he is totally housebroken. He does not go upstairs at all. Just sometimes, he slips down to the basement, and we usually don't find the mess for a couple of days. What should we do?"

"Is there a door to the basement stairs?" I asked.

"Yes."

"Close it."

I suppose we could have come up with a fancy MacGyver-style gadget that would send an alarm to a smartphone if it detected Gordon breaking the plane of the doorway to the basement. But closing the door would be easier. Just as in these two cases, proper management usually doesn't cost much in time or effort. The strategy here is, keep it simple.

Too often, I have seen ads for rehoming a dog with a phrase like, "Needs room to run." To me, such wording insinuates that nobody has properly socialized the dog. Exercise alone does not change a dog's behavior; it just tires out the dog. If exercise is offered routinely without proper socialization, it builds up the dog's stamina and his bad manners become exaggerated—she has more endurance to act out. Dogs do not require room to run before they need a properly developed and maintained relationship with a dedicated human.

Managing dogs exclusively outdoors, even if within a fenced yard, is not adequate care for most. Over my years as a professional trainer, I have received dozens of calls about dogs that act out in a myriad of ways due to unacceptable outdoor management: "Jake chewed through the siding on our house. Peaches ripped out the electrical wires under our camper. Tom-Tom dug a hole more than three feet deep—my wife fell in and tore a ligament—he's got to go!"

Here's a frequent one: "Bowser barks out there incessantly all night long." Why is Bowser left outdoors all night long? Poor Bowser—he wants to be part of the family. Putting him outside for the night is like sending your kid to bed on the back patio. I don't expect everyone to allow their dogs to sleep in their bedrooms, but a dog needs to believe he is part of the family if you expect him to present the good behaviors of a well-mannered dog. If you treat a dog like a goat, you will get a goat.

Poor management can cause damage or death to the beloved dog. It can also cause harm to humans and is a serious liability issue that many people do not consider.

When I lived in Wisconsin, a local family took in a stray dog—and by that, I mean they started to feed it off their back porch. The dog had been eating their food for just a couple of weeks when it crossed the road in front of a motorcyclist, causing an accident that led to the amputation of the driver's leg. The dog suffered a worse fate and was peeled off the pavement by the streets-and-sanitation department. A few months later, the family received notice that they were being sued for damages.

Apparently, in that county in Wisconsin, the law states that you legally own and therefore are responsible for a dog that you have maintained (feeding was considered maintaining). The settlement was for close to a million dollars, if I recall correctly. The point is that you are legally responsible for the actions of your dog, whether he is on your property at the time or not. Since it is easier to control a dog's behavior when he is under your supervision, I strongly recommend doing what is necessary to contain and control your dog.

Appropriate supervision is an offshoot of proper management. Since the fundamental four steps of socialization require that the dog's leader pay attention in order to provide necessary information about the social rules, supervision is not optional. I would venture to say that most dog behavioral issues arise due to poor supervision. When the dog doesn't receive information that a behavior is unacceptable and practices that behavior without consequence, then he forms a bad habit. Without supervision, there's no way to offer a warning to a dog about moving toward breaking a standard.

I receive many calls from people about housebreaking issues. Housebreaking requires a combination of exceptional management paired with excellent supervision. If you are not able to completely supervise a baby puppy, the pup must be confined so that it cannot get into dangerous situations and so that it will wait, while crated, to be let outdoors to potty. Raising a baby puppy requires 100 percent supervision unless the pup is safely confined.

A client told me, "Maggie doesn't poop indoors or in her crate. We are happy about that. But she still pees on the floor."

"It's important that someone is supervising her one hundred percent of the time when she is out so that you can see if she is about to potty. Often, a puppy will do a little circle movement before she pees. When that happens, do something to interrupt her, like clapping your hands. Then pick her up and take her outdoors. She may need some time to feel relaxed enough to potty again, so be patient," I explained.

"Yes, yes, we know all that. But she is still going potty in the house."

"You are one hundred percent supervising her?"

"Yes."

"So, you are watching her pee?"

"No. She goes into the spare bedroom and behind the chair in there. Sometimes we don't find it for a day. You know she is small, and the pee sometimes dries up before we find it. But then we can smell it after a while."

I saw a newspaper article about the rise in child

drownings with the increased use of large, inflatable swimming pools. It claimed, "43% of children were supervised when they drowned, 39% were not supervised and 18% of children died during a lapse in supervision." For your information, my definition of "supervision" for puppy housebreaking is inconsistent with the one the parents of the drowned children seem to have used. That is why I claim you need to 100 percent supervise a puppy that is not crated. Since parents cannot seem to 100 percent supervise their young children even around swimming pools, I strongly suggest using management—like crating a puppy when you cannot 100 percent supervise it.

In one class, I instructed students to command their dogs to lie down and stay, and a while later, a dog got up and walked over to visit with another dog. Interestingly, I had to alert the owner that her dog had gotten up and sauntered off. Since there was nothing more important in those few moments than training the dog, I am uncertain why the student did not see the dog's initial flinch to stand up and intervene at that point, well before it even moved from a down to a sit position. But, sadly, people simply do not pay attention. They chat with a fellow student, and their own dog's behavior falls in priority. Failure to supervise is an extremely critical mistake that dog owners make. It can cause so much damage to the dog or others.

#7: Misguided Methods

"Put this in front of your right eye and read line six from left to right," the nurse said.

I followed the instructions.

"Nothing wrong with your sight. Let's go to x-ray to see if there's any damage to your skull."

I was wheeled to the radiology department and endured the procedure. Then I was returned to the examining room, where my husband sat in the corner. More than a few minutes later, a doctor entered. "No fracture," he said. "We can just get that cut sutured up, and you can be on your way. Shouldn't be more than five or six stitches, and I can hide most of them close to your eyebrow. You won't have too much of a scar." He pressed the flesh over my occipital lobe together with a little less sensitivity than I would have liked. Then he asked, "Can you explain what caused the injury?"

This would be my third time telling the story to hospital staff—first in reception, next with the nurse, now with the doctor. My husband glanced my way at the doctor's question. I was beginning to think he was right. On our way in to the ER, he had commented, "They are going to think that I hit you—that this is a domestic assault—because you were struck in the eye."

"That's ridiculous," I had replied. "Look at my condition. It's obvious I was working with sheep!" That part was true: I had sheep dung in my boots. My jeans told the story of falling where livestock had been, including a bit of hay in my pockets and a smeared stain on my hip of what could only be identified as poop. I emitted that sheepy-goaty smell.

Jane had scheduled sheep-herding lessons with me via e-mail. She lived about ninety minutes away in a university town and had two Border Collies that were apparently highly competitive in the sport of Flyball. That did not impress me. The dogs were named Trouble and Mayhem. That impressed me even less. Who would do that? Her e-mail signature suggested that she should have been a bit intelligent.

Over my ten years of giving livestock-herding lessons, I had seen a dramatic drop in the general obedience and self-restraint of my students' dogs. I attributed it to the surge in popularity of Agility, a sport that should not have caused the demise of sound dog training. However, it arose at the same time as clicker training, which served Agility competitors well. In some ways, the two became entwined.

Trick training, which I define as teaching behaviors that are not inherently natural for dogs, is typically best accomplished using positive-reinforcement techniques. Clicker training is a positive-reinforcement method that adds a bridge (the sound of the click) to the reinforcer (the food) so that the dog can receive information that he did right before the actual reward is delivered. Agility can be described as a string of tricks along a steeplechase-type course. Clicker training is a great option when a dog is working at a distance from the handler. So, clicker training and Agility were a sort of match made in doggie heaven.

Even though Agility is a timed event, the dog must keep composure. There are contact zones on some obstacles that the dog has to touch and it may not knock down jump bars. The dog needs to remain still, without restraint of a leash, before the run begins. Additionally, the dog must remain in communication with his handler in order to run the course in the right sequence. He must take commands while running quite fast. High standards of obedience to authority can truly benefit its competitors.

At the dawn of both Agility and clicker training, I was a busy scientist in corporate America. Every day, I commuted over seventy miles each way—I worked near a large city but lived on a little farm where I raised sheep so that I could feed my passion to train Border Collies for herding competitions. I simply didn't have the extra time to delve into Agility.

I had used positive-reinforcement methods for years, side by side with correction-based training. In this, I was not alone. Many of my fellow obedience-club members did the same, integrating the two methods seamlessly. If we wanted to teach a dog to perform a desired behavior, we often used food or toy rewards. If we needed to remedy an unacceptable behavior, we used corrections.

The number of herding clients whose dogs were unruly seemed to be increasing, but I did not immediately relate it to clicker training or positive reinforcement. It was not until someone suggested that dog training had to be limited exclusively to positive-reinforcement techniques that the world began to implode. The idea caught on like wildfire, burning down the reliable structure of reasonable, practical, logical, and judicious dog training. In time, I began to consider the philosophy a cult, because websites promoting it advocated attacking, shunning, and bullying people who chose to use corrections. There has now even been a push for legislation against certain correction-based training techniques and tools. As I experienced it, the evolution of the all-positive-reinforcement movement led to a rapid increase in antisocial dogs—dogs that had little or no respect for their humans.

The day that Jane arrived with Trouble and Mayhem, I knew we were in for both trouble and mayhem. The dogs each jumped from her vehicle and raced to the end of a tight leash. Jane leaned back to first shoulder the jerk and then to counterbalance the heaving draw. The dogs focused on the objective of their choice and pulled Jane, like a team of sled dogs, toward it. They had fixed their lasers on the pen of sheep for the lesson.

The parking area was about 150 feet from the herding arenas. Jane was hauled that great distance, displaying no evidence that she thought she should correct her dogs' intractable behavior. The sheep communicated their sentiments about the new students by bunching into a tight cluster. The most mature ewe scuffed the dirt with her front hoof and snorted. I knew this could be disastrous.

Dealing with livestock can be hazardous. Several different species can be herded. With cattle, the most common strategy is to drive them. Cattle are big animals. It is prudent to pressure them to move ahead of the cowboy (who may be mounted on a horse or ATV) and his canine. If the cattle begin to race away, the dog or horseman can run out and head them off, turn them back, and return them to the desired path. But, for the most part, the dog and/or human remains behind the herd. It's safer that way.

With sheep, it is more customary for a shepherd (human) to walk or ride at the head of the lot. The dog fetches the livestock up to the person. This behavior is instinctive in many breeds, and it starts with the dog attempting to get to the head of the flock to turn the animals toward the handler. When that happens in a smaller space, the dog tends to circle the stock because a straight course is impossible. The trainer can use the dog's motivation to get to the head of the stock to teach it to change flanks (directions) around the sheep. It's a good place to instruct the dog how to yield to pressure from the shepherd as well. Working in a small space can facilitate helping a dog to find the balance point and come to a stop. For these reasons, I often started new dogs in a space about fifty by fifty feet. It kept the whole process safely contained and allowed the dog a chance to "win" by locating the balance point and stopping there, all beneficial in early herding lessons.

The detriment of working in a small arena, though, is that there is no room to escape—for the sheep, the dog, or the human. One must rely on livestock that are accustomed to being worked by a dog. This method also requires a dog to have some level of obedience to authority. It needs to understand the concept of receiving a correction, so that the handler can influence the dog if things begin to go awry. When an inexperienced dog is first exposed to sheep, it may become so excited by the lighting up of its instincts that it may attempt to run in and grab a sheep. If the dog has been trained to respect a human authority figure, it is far more likely to yield to pressure from that person and regain its senses. A dog that has never learned to revere a human could be an utterly treacherous pupil.

It became obvious, in the first few sentences of my conversation with Jane, that Trouble and Mayhem had never received a correction. Worse, Jane was staunchly opposed to delivering a consequence for unruly behavior. When I asked her why, she insisted that correcting a dog would cause it to lose speed on the Flyball course.

The sport of Flyball became popular around the same time as Agility. Teams compete side by side in relays in which each dog in turn jumps four hurdles, hits a box that releases a tennis ball, catches the ball, and then goes back over the same hurdles to the start/finish line. Unlike Agility, where a variety of obstacles can be presented at different trials, Flyball is fairly invariable. There are four jumps; there is the box with the ball. It's a game that encourages a bit of wild abandon and extreme speed, and it can incite an obsessive-compulsive behavior in some dogs. Unlike Agility, in Flyball, the dogs may be physically restrained until released. There really isn't much need to foster a dog's self-restraint.

Regardless of the games that its owner chooses for them to play, a dog must be social. It must have some manners. It needs to be sufficiently compliant to exist in human society without being a nuisance.

I struggled to understand Jane's perspective. I also grappled with the notion of going into a pen of sheep with a dog that had no sense of conceding to authority. As I've noted, for ten years, I had seen the degradation of dog etiquette with subsequent herding students. I felt as if I had reached the point of no return. I did not want to subject Jane or myself to the dangers of taking dogs like Trouble and Mayhem into an arena of innocent but potentially contentious ewes.

I drew a line in the sand. "Jane, herding is dangerous. You need to show me that your dog will listen to you, that it won't pull on the leash as we move toward the gate of the pen. The sheep have already sized up your dog. But if he can walk to the gate under self-restraint, sit or lie down on the outside of the gate, refrain from racing into the pen when we open the gate, and walk in calmly when we invite him into the pen, I am willing to proceed. Can you demonstrate that level of control over your dog?"

"Just because I don't use corrections doesn't mean that I never trained my dogs. They are obedient to me," she replied.

I was speechless for a moment. I remained calm,

took in a deep breath, and then said, "OK. Before we go in to work your dog, please show me that he will walk on a loose lead and sit or down on a verbal command, and that you can reach for the gate handle without him going crazy."

"Sure. I will probably not be able to work Mayhem today because he's only two years old and still a baby."

"OK..." was all I could utter. Two years old is not still a baby!

Of course, Jane's demonstration was an epic failure. Trouble could not take one step forward without lunging. He didn't respond to her verbal commands of "sit" or "down." Jane asked if she could go back to the car to get some treats. I obliged because I knew what the outcome would be. As I had expected, the treats didn't change Trouble's lack of obedience. He had targeted those sheep milling about in the pen. They obviously represented many more motivational units than a jerky treat.

Then the angels sang. "What, exactly, do you mean when you say that you need to correct a dog?"

I hadn't been expecting that. I suppose Jane had assumed the next thing out of my mouth would be, "See you later; nice knowing you." So, to keep her options open, she'd taken the risk of sounding ignorant. She was right that I had been about to pull the rip cord. But I honored her choice to learn something other than herding that day.

After I explained much of what you've learned here about the four steps of canine socialization, the use of a correction collar, and having the right presence—which is worth more than the cost of a herding lesson—Jane cocked her head. "Do you think that could really work to get Trouble under control?"

The choir of angels caroled gilded notes of joy. The sky was opening up. Through the clouds, I could see streaks of sunlight filtering down to earth, illuminating the ground on which we stood. "Yes."

"So, is that something *you* can do?"

"Yes. I can do it right now."

Jane stood by while I adjusted a collar on her dog's neck—up high, where a correction collar should sit. I bent down and attached a light leash, because the one she was using had been designed to control a horse. I didn't need the power of the leash to control her dog. As I stood up, Trouble did exactly what I had predicted: he lunged to the end of the leash. When one removes a very heavy lead and replaces it with something much lighter, the dog often feels that the leash is no longer attached and is compelled to escape the drudgery of constant tension on his neck.

I was ready; I held tight. Trouble got to the end of the leash, and he nearly flipped backward because he wasn't actually off lead. He yelped out of sheer surprise. I remained standing calmly. He looked at me, something he had never done to his owner. Then he came back into my "zone." I feigned forward movement. Trouble leaped forward again, and he endured the same result. That time, he didn't yelp. I have learned that dogs are more apt to bark out of surprise than pain.

Trouble returned to my space and sat. I pretended to take another small step. I couldn't fool him. What did I expect? He was a Border Collie. They are not easily fooled twice. At that moment—after just two corrections—Trouble's life changed. The angst that had been painted on his face and controlled his whole body dissipated. He began to breathe normally. The tension in his muscles eased. He observed his world rather than scrutinized it.

I began to walk. Trouble measured his pace. I turned right; he followed. I turned left; he yielded space to let me in. I stopped. He sat—not because I had given him a command, but because he realized that I would determine when and where we traveled.

I worked with Trouble another ten minutes. I took him to the gate of the pen of sheep and reached for the handle. He took the bait and tried to beat me through the opening. I said the word "wait" and gave him a sharp, snappy correction. He looked up at me with understanding. We walked away from the pen and then returned to the gate. I reached for the handle. He sat back. I took that moment to reach down and touch him for the first time—a gentle stroke over his head. It was the first time I spoke to him—with a calm, soothing "Good boy."

It was then that I felt that we could proceed with the herding lesson—not because I had done all that was necessary to resolve Trouble's trouble, but because I saw that the dog had a conscience. I felt that he recognized me as an authority figure he could trust.

I explained the rules to Jane. "The sheep know me. They will gravitate to me in the presence of a dog. Your dog knows you. He will probably choose to work the sheep toward you. Therefore, you and I must be one entity. We cannot move apart. If you cannot stick with me, you may find me reaching for your arm and linking elbows with you. It's critical that we give a unified image to the sheep and dog."

It did not surprise me that as soon as Jane entered the picture, Trouble turned into his old self. But I had the leash, and I corrected him for acting stupid—because that is what he was doing, and he knew it as soon as he felt the consequence. He shot me a look of apology. As we moved into the pen, there were a few blips of frivolity that required adjustment, but because I had taught him earlier to lie down on a verbal command, he obliged after a single correction.

Next, I explained to Jane that she should stand by the sheep. I would move Trouble as far from them as possible and then calmly remove the leash. I told her that as soon as I released her dog, I would quickly move to her side. That would give the dog and sheep the best chance to establish the positions we hoped to achieve. Fortunately, Trouble remained down long enough for me to get next to Jane and be prepared to help him to begin circling behind the sheep. He yielded to my pressure when I stepped to block his path. He changed flanks. Jane struggled to stick by my side. I moved backward toward the fence to present a balance point for her dog. Trouble felt it and turned in. I stepped to the side to encourage a wide flank around the sheep and us. Jane did not follow, so I grabbed for her hand to bring her closer, but she bobbed and went the other way.

I explained my injury to the emergency-room doctor. "The dog was new to herding. He started the lesson fairly well for his lack of general obedience. He had a rather incompetent owner—she was supposed to stay next to me so that the sheep would be drawn to the two of us and not split up."

The doctor was on the edge of losing attention.

"Jane and I were separated, and then she stumbled backward and fell down. That caused her dog to lose any semblance of self-control, and the sheep split up. The dog took the chance for a cheap shot and ran into the packet of three ewes that had raced to be next to me. One sheep ran into the back of my knees and knocked me to my butt—so now, Jane and I were both on our asses. Three ewes were right behind me, and the fourth was fifteen feet in front. He had been separated from his flock, and there was a crazy dog in the pen. He took the most direct route back to the herd—which just happened to be through my head!"

I am fairly certain that Robert could drop any worries about the domestic-assault accusation. My story was far too strange not to be true.

That sheep had panicked and had had no choice but to go through me to reach his destination. I will never forget the look in his eyes. The look on the doctor's face was eerily similar.

Jane's reluctance to use a correction to train her dogs was rooted in propaganda from the all-positive-reinforcement movement. She had been taught the puffery that her dog would not run fast if he received corrections for unacceptable behavior. Nothing could be further from the truth.

Speed, whether in an Agility, Flyball, or herding arena, materializes when the dog feels confident. Confidence comes from trust in the handler and the dog's feelings about his own competence. It is a result of sound training, specifically for accuracy. Herding dogs must run fast—faster than a flock of sheep or a runaway cow. My experience tells me that initial lessons should be designed to assist a dog to feel successful. Using the right-size arena, well-dog-broke sheep, and scenarios set up so she can win and outrun her charges are all very valuable in developing a dog's confidence. On the contrary, if you begin a dog's herding training in a large space where the livestock can outrun the dog, the dog's confidence drops, and he may quit trying.

If you help a dog achieve the mission, you get speed as a fringe benefit. It is important to teach a dog that he can rely on you and that he can trust your judgment. Training for speed by refraining from correcting mistakes can lead to a dog that feels defeated. Defeat does not foster speed. Regardless of what sport you play, your dog will be happiest if he knows what your expectations are so that he can behave within the limits to please you. Then, speed is a natural by-product of that system.

One of the most common mistakes that dog owners make is to believe that it is possible to raise a well-adjusted, mannerly dog without using appropriate corrections. Positive reinforcement is designed to create good behavior. Receiving unpleasant consequences resolves undesirable behavior. Both methods are necessary to nurture a companion dog. Failing to use the power of positive reinforcement reduces a dog's opportunity to experiment and be creative in training solutions. It limits the dog's capacity to present the vastness of his potential to perform useful tasks. However, failing to implement the four steps of canine socialization results in a dog that cannot truly trust, is deprived of recognizing social boundaries, and fails to fit into your family because he continually behaves outside of your expectations. The fallout of that situation can often be disappointment, frustration, and anger. It can result in unfair treatment of a dog that is given no guidance for behaving properly—within the boundaries of his owner's expectations.

#8: Suspecting Sabotage

Amelia Earhart said, "The most effective way to do it, is to do it."

I have heard clients say things like, "Everything was going well with Smitty until we went on vacation and my mom took care of him for a week. Since then, he's just back to his old, bad behavior."

Or, "I'm the one doing all the work with Molly. The kids don't work with her, and my husband just ruins everything when he gets home. It's impossible for me to keep her from being naughty because of my family."

I've heard, "When I take Cooper for a walk by myself, I can pretty much keep him next to me, but I think he thinks he's allowed to pull when my neighbor comes along, because her dog, Jackson, pulls terribly."

Another client told me, "If it weren't for my brother coming in late at night after work, everything would be great with Sinbad. But Joe just spoils him and gives him human food from his late-night dinner. It's pretty much impossible to keep Sinbad behaving right because of my brother's influence."

Then there was, "When I am home, Becker is perfect. But when I'm at work, the kids leave the gate open when they get home from school, and Becker gets out. Or they don't let him go potty outside, and he pees in the house. I think there's no hope."

Excuses, excuses!

While I can understand that all these clients feel hopeless and out of control of their situations, that's only because...they are hopelessly out of control of their situations. The answer is simply to get back in control. Some of these examples require a shift in management; others require a shift in perspective. Some require both.

Under most situations, a dog's behavior is a reflection of its relationship with the humans in its life. Let's consider a bunch of school kids. When they are with bus driver Alice, they are well mannered and remain fairly quiet on the ride to school. When they are with bus driver Mary, they are unruly, noisy, and disruptive. When six-year-old Megan is with Grandma Jones, she is sweet, compliant, and obedient. When she is with Grandma Johnson, she is a hellion. It's the same person but in different relationships. Kids can behave differently with one parent than the other, one teacher than another, or one coach than another. Dogs present the same phenomenon.

It doesn't really matter that Smitty spent time with his owner's parents. They may not set standards for his behavior when they are responsible for him, but that has little to do with the relationship that he has with his owners. If Mom or Dad permitted Smitty to bark out the window—a behavior that isn't allowed at his own house—then, sure, he may try it when he gets home. But if the standard was previously set and enforced, it should only take a quick intervention to remind Smitty of it. If he was behaving at a specific standard before the vacation, it should not take long to bring him back into calibration when he rejoins good leaders.

Smitty's case is pretty simple because he is removed from the toxic relationship he has with the "grandparents." Once he is back on home turf, reminding him about previously established standards should be fairly easy, as long as his owner remains calm and presents an aura of authority rather than frustration vibes about her bad-dog-owner parents.

10 Most Common Mistakes Dog Owners Make

On the contrary, Molly's owner must experience a daily dose of disobedient children and an uncooperative husband. Notice that I did not mention Molly's behavior, because that is truly not the thorn in Molly's owner's side. Jane is irritated that her kids won't listen to her. My response is, "I am a dog trainer, not a child psychologist. If you want me to fix your kids, it is going to cost a lot more." If she asks me to fix her husband's behavior, I assure her that she can't afford it.

I recommend that someone like Jane ignore what she cannot control and that she lead by example. First, she needs to set the standards for Molly. Then she needs to reinforce them, no matter what else is going on around her. She should consider her children and husband as distractions in the environment that she can use to remind Molly to obey the rules regardless of what is happening in the world. There's no difference between the presence of a kid and a squirrel. If Molly is told to sit and stay, she needs to do that whether the kids are playing ball or a cat walks into the room.

I asked Jane what she meant when she said that her husband ruined everything. She stated that the rule is no jumping up, but Bill slaps his thighs and encourages Molly to jump on him. I explained that she must tell her husband that he gets to pick one *or* the other.

Let's say that Jane and Bill take option one: jumping on someone is a standard that they set. As the dog's owner, if Bill wants Molly to jump on him, he gives her a command to do so. He is the only one that she may jump on, and Jane doesn't intervene. However, she is not permitted to jump on anyone else, and Jane is to intervene if she sees Molly about to jump on anyone, including Bill if he doesn't use the correct command word.

Or, they can take option two: Molly should not jump on anyone, and if Bill encourages her to jump on him, Jane intervenes and corrects her for jumping anyway. It's not a very fair option, but that is the point of presenting it to Bill. He needs to understand that his behavior is unjust to Molly and to Jane, as her leader.

I understand that some people like their dogs to jump on them, but I don't think dogs should be permitted to jump on anyone who has not given a command to do so. Additionally, I don't think it's prudent to permit a dog to believe she can jump on someone other than her owner, even if he or she encourages the dog to do so.

The most important point that Jane needed to hear was that nobody can sabotage her relationship with Molly. She was capable of establishing an excellent relationship with her dog and might have to consider her kids as an outside distraction. I warned her against telling her children, "When Molly does this or that behavior, you need to do this or that to Molly," because they have shown no interest in participating in the dog's training, and Jane claims that she can't make them. Therefore, she needs to focus on the only person she can control, and that is herself.

Cooper's owner, James, believed that his neighbor's dog was sabotaging Cooper's understanding of the no-pulling rule. Excuse! Red flag number one: James said that he can "pretty much *keep Cooper next to him*" during the walk. James needs to read, "#3: Permitting Pulling." Resolving a pulling issue is not about teaching the dog to stay in a specific zone, it is about instructing him that he may not assume the leadership role in the relationship. Once a dog understands that idea, and if the owner maintains the relationship hierarchy properly (as in, the human is the leader and the dog is the follower), then Cooper's main focus in life should be to work within the standards set by his benevolent leader. In the same way that Jane could consider her kids an outside distraction, James's behavior should be to remind Cooper that he may not trigger on outside influences.

We humans often blame some outside event for our struggles; this always results in a lack of success. We must focus on what we can control. We should be grateful for dogs like Jackson, for squirrels, and for naughty kids because they give us daily opportunities to remind our dogs about our expectations. If we can expose them to such interruptions often, the level of intervention required to remind them of our expectations doesn't have to be very intense. That creates a highly predicable world for the dog, and he can trust that we will remind him when he is about to slip past a boundary that we have set. We become a very important person to our dog—one that he relies upon to keep him safe from falling off the wagon of compliance. He can frequently please us, which means that he feels forever safe with his position in our society. He feels welcome and cherished because we are paying attention to him and helping him at all times.

Sinbad's owner, Charlotte, may need to revamp her evening management strategy. It's impossible to supervise a dog when you are sleeping. Perhaps she could resolve the whole issue by keeping Sinbad in her closed bedroom at night. Or, she could consider having him sleep in a crate. We have already learned that we cannot control other people. If Charlotte doesn't want Sinbad to eat food that her brother may share, she needs to provide a management system to address the issue.

When I offered that option to Charlotte, she said that she felt that her brother's behavior was teaching Sinbad to beg for food. Remember that the overriding principle in this chapter is that the relationship that you form with your dog will not be easily corrupted by others as long as you do what is necessary to maintain rapport with her. There's little need to focus on outside incidents unless they become a danger for your dog. I don't disapprove of feeding a dog "human" food. I think that most of it is at least as good for a dog, if not better, than commercially processed dog-food products. Just because a dog is offered human-grade food does not mean that he will become a begging dog. A dog becomes a beggar when he is given food—any food—when he begs. For that reason, it is not prudent to offer food to a drooling dog that is piercing you with his gaze.

However, even if one person rewards a begging behavior, if others refrain from doing so, a dog will not beg from them. My husband is likely to give our dogs a last morsel off his plate, yet I almost never do that. My dogs never beg from me, but of course they hang out by him in case he decides to offer them something. Again, a dog's behavior is a direct reflection of its relationship with the human(s) in its life. Charlotte could resolve her problem by managing her dog away from her brother's influence, since she is asleep when the unacceptable behavior occurs. Alternatively, she could permit her brother to share a snack with Sinbad, realizing that it won't turn Sinbad into a beggar-in-general unless others offer food for that behavior as well.

Becker's owner is complaining about her kids' bad

influence over the dog. By this time, it should be obvious what I would recommend: because her kids won't follow her instructions, Becker should be left in a crate until she gets home from work. If she said that was too long to ask a dog to remain crated, I would ask if she can instruct at least one child to take Becker outside for a potty break, making certain that the gate latch is closed, and recrate him afterward. She insists that her kids won't comply, though; so we are back to square one: the crate.

Many people will protest that all-day crating seems unfair to a dog, but one alternative is that he gets hit by a car on his way to the neighbor's house. Worse, he might cause some sort of an injury to others while he is loose. Sometimes we just have to put all the cards on the table and evaluate what we have. Complaining on a daily basis that the world is happening to you is just not a great way to exist.

Many dog owners fail to focus on their relationship with the dog and choose to blame the outside world for its naughty behavior. The world is not on a quest to sabotage you. A dog's behavior is a reflection of his relationship with his owner, so focus on that and on what you can control. Your dog will thank you for shedding all your frustration and anger baggage and putting his needs higher on your priority list.

#9: Tenderness before Trust

When I was seventeen years old, I spent a year in Johannesburg, South Africa, as a foreign-exchange student. The first day, my host mother and sister greeted me with warmth and kindness. We went directly to the shop that sold school uniforms, as I would attend my new high school the very next day. That was new for me, as US public schools did not require uniforms. I wondered how I would adjust.

With new winter and summer outfits, I was then introduced to my room in a beautiful, sprawling expanse of a house. All my life, I had shared a room with my little sister, so I was thrilled to have my very own space with a bed, built-in desk, and lots of closet room. I was instructed to leave my school shoes outside my door each evening to be shined by Freddy. I had never worn shoes that needed to be shined, and I had certainly never experienced having domestic help. Then my mum gestured toward a large brown towel that lay neatly folded on the bed. "That's your bath towel," she said. I nodded.

I was introduced to the palatial bath that the five children shared, and then the rest of the house. I was treated like a beloved relative—more than a guest—and I drank it all in, along with that splendid South African accent that I could not get enough of. My host sister was thrilled to have a female sibling, as she was a girly girl who was into ballet, dance, and fashion. She had endured the wrath of four brothers and hoped I would help tip the gender scale a bit. While we did slowly develop a very good relationship, I found having brothers fun and exciting, something that I do not think Diane appreciated much.

About ten days later, after I had just begun to adjust to my new family, new school, new friends, and my new life, my sister stopped into my room after school. "Tammie, you know we love you. We adore having you here," she started in that elegant accent. I sensed that her tone was not wholly consistent with her words, and I felt my stomach grumble. "But, Tam, you just must understand. You must stop using everyone else's towel." I could hear disappointment, frustration, and a trace of anger in her words, and I felt as if I were two feet tall.

Although the home I had grown up in was not nearly as expansive as the beautiful home in South Africa, my mother had kept our house tidy and comfy. She was an artistic person who had a keen eye for color, and my father owned a paint and decorating shop. Mom wasn't a fashion czar, but she was cognizant of color and patterns and shared her knowledge with us. I recall her explaining the fashion faux pas of wearing brown shoes with a black belt or mixing stripes with plaids.

The bathroom that my two sisters and I shared was well beautified with festive wallpaper (from my father's store) and nice fixtures. Most important, the towels matched the decor. All of the towels were the same color, save the little hand towels that were draped over the larger bath towels. They were of a complimentary color and "just for decoration," not to be used to dry our hands. After a shower, we were to hang our bath towel over the tub's curtain rod to dry. Then, every day, my mother would do a load of laundry and wash our towels. There were extra towels in the linen closet. They were all color coordinated by room. My parents' bathroom was a different color, so their towels coordinated with that decor. There were strict orders about how to handle laundry so that none was left lying on the floor. This was all to support my mother, who spent most of her day making our house a wonderful home.

On my first day in South Africa, I did not appreciate that the drab, brown towel on my bed was specifically my own. I did think it odd that the massive kids' bathroom was filled with entirely mismatched bath accessories. Not one of the towels matched another. Some had patterns; others were solid. None complemented another. To my eyes, it made for a very disjointed, inharmonious room that shouted "boy's gym." My mother would have cringed at seeing such a space. I simply figured that boys just had no sense of fashion or style.

My father was a businessman who left the house each morning in a newly pressed dress shirt, suit, and tie. He wasn't the kind of guy who could teach me how "boys" acted. I chalked up the South Africa bath-towel situation to an insignificant but gender-specific difference. But now I was hearing that I'd had it all wrong.

My South African sister was trying to be gentle with me, but beneath her kind words, I could hear the disdain for my wretched behavior. I tried to comprehend what she was saying. Just like I would have done in the home where I grew up, when I stepped out of the shower, I reached for any clean towel and dried off. Imagine, however, if towels were personal items, like toothbrushes or pairs of underwear.

I began to sense how my sister felt when she went into the bath and "her" exclusive towel was wet and spent—used by that mannerless American kid. I felt ashamed, guilty, and stupid. Thoughts raced through my mind. How could I have known that when my mum pointed out my towel, it was *my* towel? It was outside of my reality to consider towels with such personal attachment.

For three days before I flew to Johannesburg, the

American Field Service held training sessions in New York City for the thirty-one of us who would be traveling there. We did exercises designed to help us understand what it might be like to live in a new culture, but none of them had mentioned towels. I felt naked in my ignorance. But once I knew the rule, it was easy to shift my behavior and fit into my new family's expectation for bathroom etiquette. This was only the first of many lessons I've learned about living in a foreign country.

Basically, I discovered that there are some things that all humans have in common, regardless of whether they live in a mud hut or a palace. And some things are unique not just to a particular country but also to regions within one or to neighborhoods within a city. The most important thing I learned is to honor differences, because they are what make each of us unique and special. They are not bad; they are just different.

It has been over thirty years since I lived in Johannesburg. Yet, I recall so many moments as if it were yesterday. I have been fortunate enough to have studied emerald toucanets in the cloud forest in Monteverde, Costa Rica; lived for six years in a really big city; worked in corporate America; purchased a home as a single woman; raised sheep on a farm; trained Border Collies for herding competitions, and even though I got married, created two companies, survived two national economic crises as a small business owner, I still consider my time in South Africa as the most influential year of my life.

I find it fitting that the lessons I learned about cultural differences have crossed species and into the way that I understand dogs. As mammals and as social carnivores, they are very much like us humans in some very basic and obvious ways. And yet, as canine, they are unique too. Dogs have their own culture, one could say. Yet, we ask them to live in our realm.

I suspect that dogs often face the "towel dilemma" during their cohabitation with people. I can imagine a nice dog that is sure he's doing just fine, and then he's hit with his owner's disappointment, frustration, or anger but doesn't have a clue how to fix the situation. Just like I felt as a teenager living with strangers halfway around the world, dogs want to fit in and be accepted into their human family. They are motivated toward membership in the collective over a solitary life not by choice but by genetic influence. It's as if they are all enrolled in a "foreign-exchange program" the moment their new families come to pick them out of the litter; however, they don't get the three-day training session before they embark on their new adventure.

In this book, I share my experiences of living with dogs and the people who claim them as beloved family members. Nearly all my clients tell me that they love their dogs. But what does that mean? Love sometimes requires doing what is best for the dog, even if it doesn't feel good to do it. I don't think it was comfortable for my host sister to confront me about my bath-towel etiquette either. But had she not, I could never have corrected my behavior and would have spent a year irritating my host family until they labeled me a hopeless failure, unable to learn simple tasks and show the most basic level of comportment. They would have been happy that they only had to stick it out for a year and bid me adieu.

When a client is explaining her dog's issues, it's not uncommon for her to toss in the phrase, "Don't get me wrong, I really love my dog," before continuing with the laundry list of unacceptable behaviors. I don't have an issue with the list per se. Dogs do jump up, pull on the leash, scratch people, refuse commands, run off, growl, and even bite. I expect to hear the list, since the client is bringing the dog to me for training and social rehabilitation. What I find curious is how often people feel a need to temper their comments with their love for the dog—as if it is unloving to describe a dog's behavioral issues.

Empathy and compassion are building blocks of love, both as we relate to other humans and our dogs. But love also requires the tough stuff—like conversations about towels. It's not enough to say words at a dog and expect him to understand them. It's critical that we evaluate whether he has an awareness of our expectations. The best way to do that is to use the four steps of socialization: establishing standards, paying attention, offering the warning, and, when necessary, following up with a consequence.

My understanding of dogs tells me that they are more like children under two years old: they need direct feedback—no negotiation, no assumptions. When we are clear and deliberate, the dog can trust us. Before a dog can feel your compassion and empathy, which is how *you* may experience love, he must trust you. Setting standards and reinforcing them is the best way to let your dog know that he can rely on you to be predictable. Predictability precedes trust.

A very common mistake that dog owners make is to put love before trust. Perhaps it is better to say that a common mistake that dog owners make is to misunderstand how dogs perceive love. Either way, in my experience, sticking to the four steps of socialization offers your dog the best opportunity to use the right towels in your house. That means that he can trust you, which is how a dog probably feels your love at the most basic level. It also means that he can please you, and that is how he shows his love to you.

#10: Shortsighted Selection

You can't choose your relatives, but you can choose your dog. Poor selection is a very common mistake that dog owners make—and it is the easiest to control. I suspect most people spend more time deciding what brand of refrigerator to purchase than what sort of dog they want to live with for the next fifteen years. Since you can review your lifestyle against the general disposition of hundreds of breeds and mixes of dogs, failure to make the right choice is a mistake that shouldn't happen.

In Appendix C, I have added information on how to evaluate breeds based on two critical attributes: biddability and work drive. Once you know these basic qualities of a breed, you can compare it to your lifestyle and expectations for your relationship with your next dog. It is a valuable evaluation.

Let's contemplate breed differences. Breeds are different because they were very specifically designed to perform unique tasks. Through the process of artificial selection, dog breeds have become highly distinctive. It may not seem a very important endeavor today, especially when every Tom, Dick, or Harry can create a "designer" breed that has no intended purpose. However, when breeds were constructed historically, there was a dedicated person or group of people who were highly motivated to make the best dog possible for their specific needs. They made tough decisions and culled dogs from the breeding program that didn't meet the standards they had set. The fact that as a single woman, I could manage a flock of sixty sheep without help from another human was because some devoted farmers in Scotland and Wales once dedicated themselves to developing the Border Collie over a hundred years ago. With one dog, I was able to do the work of at least a few people, and without the need for sophisticated fencing and sorting chutes.

Breeds are inspired by unique motivators. scent hounds are driven to follow the trail of prey species like rabbits or raccoons. Sight hounds are triggered by the movement of their quarry. Herding breeds ache to contain or control livestock. Setters and pointers identify birds for their human hunters, while retrievers fetch them up. Livestock-guarding breeds have a strong natural tendency to bond to their shepherd's flocks and warn away predators. Terriers have a formidable desire to hunt vermin (a kitten will do in a pinch). A sled dog runs away from its owner, not toward him or her—which is a good thing if it is connected to a sled. A Newfoundland may be highly driven to prevent a child from swimming in deep water.

What does all this mean in today's world when few dogs are given the opportunity to perform their intended purposes? You must remember that instinct trumps desire to please in breeds that still possess the work ethic of their ancestors. If you want a Beagle, you will probably have to be exceptional at dog management. Hounds are not all that concerned about their owners being the best leaders. Their work, that thing deep inside them that inspires them to greatness, only requires that their owner open the gate so that they can catch the scent and trail their quarry. If you want to keep a hound, you need a fenced yard or to walk the dog on a leash, especially if there are any rabbits in the neighborhood. This requirement of ownership can be a deal breaker for those who want to hike with an untethered dog.

If you are drawn to the regal elegance of a sight hound such as an Afghan Hound, Saluki, or even a Whippet, your dog is likely to feel it is necessary to chase a squirrel now and again. Sight hounds are typically quite calm indoors, which is something that folks find curious, since they can be large dogs. They can make great companions even in an apartment. They also tend to be quiet; however, it seems almost criminal to deny them the joy of running full out in a large open area at least once in a while. Therefore, one must plan to provide such diversions for these hounds.

Terriers are small and compact, so one might think they would make great dogs for small spaces. However, pound for pound, they are exceedingly more active than most dogs. They are motivated to hunt—the prey could be a squeaky toy or a rat—and their minds seem to process tiny movements in the environment at breakneck speed. Having been designed to go into the dark recesses of a wild animal's lair, terriers sometimes lack the inclination to pay attention to a human while on the hunt. For that reason, a good terrier isn't always a great listener. Imagine having your head down a badger hole while trying to comprehend your owner's commands. Living with a terrier can be a wild roller-coaster ride of constant activity and fun, but if you expect your dog to present a heavy dose of natural obedience to your authority, you may be continually annoyed with your little dog.

If you prefer partnering with a dog that wants to do complex work at a high standard, a herding breed may right for you. Mostly, if they are raised and trained right, these are breeds that can go on a hike with you, sans the leash, and will stick around and check back with you on the journey. However, they have been designed to pit their own bodies against that of a cow with a calf or a rank bull, so you better be a great leader. If you call the wrong command in such a dangerous situation, the dog, or you, could be seriously injured. That can cause some dogs to lose their trust in your leadership. Some of the herding breeds consider any work to be a very serious endeavor—including recreation that you consider "fun." If you do not recognize that your Belgian Malinois is judging your ability to throw a Frisbee so that she can catch it at her exceedingly high standard of perfection, you may disappoint your dog! However, the upside of this is a dog that is incredibly easy to train if you use kind but clear methods.

I find it sad when I realize that the primary reason a person is seeking training advice is a complete mismatch of breed and human personality. This can be avoided before the dog and person forge a relationship. Nobody wants to give up on their dog, so it is important to adjust to the quirks or nuances of the one you select. We can't extract a dog's personality from it just because we don't get along with it. We must be honest with ourselves and realize that our own temperament is often difficult to alter, especially when we are under stress. Since there are hundreds of choices for your next best buddy, taking the time to find the right match seems like a reasonable thing to do.

It is worthwhile to go on a tangent at this point to discuss the difference between a dog's inherent personality and its behavior. I believe that puppies are hardwired to be social and each has a unique personality. I think that, at times, people confuse those two things. Some dog owners grant a puppy undue liberty because they think that behavior is part of the dog's personality and something they cannot change. Others don't take into consideration a dog's innate personality when they work with it and expect the dog to conform to a training regimen that may have worked for a previous pet but is ill-suited for the new dog's intrinsic temperament. The former (failing to address unacceptable behavior, assuming it cannot be changed) is likely to create an antisocial dog. The latter (failing to consider the dog's distinctive nature) is apt to create a dog that cannot reach its true potential or a generally unhappy dog that cannot figure out how to please you.

Let's contemplate a human family with three kids. One is a bookworm who loves to remain in her room, reading and studying; one is a very gregarious, sporty boy who is outdoors with many pals most of the time, and the third loves to stick around with his mom in the kitchen, especially when she is cooking. The three kids are very different in the way that they approach life—in what motivates them, what makes them happy. But the parents are still responsible to make certain that all three kids are appropriately social.

When Aunt Lois comes for a visit, the mother must coax the bookworm downstairs to greet her relative. She has to drag the athlete from the backyard and his friends. The third child was waiting for his aunt with a plate of cookies that he baked especially for her. There's nothing wrong or right, good or bad, about any of the three kids' natural tendencies when it comes to visits from relatives. However, the house rules are that all the kids must at least greet their relatives and spend some time with the family during their visits. They must treat guests with kindness, use good grammar when speaking, set the table, sit with good posture when eating, use their napkins, clear the table, and wash the dishes—whatever the parents define as good manners. This is what it means to be social: to learn the rules of the society and then behave within those confines because a higher-ranking one expects that sort of behavior.

Each child's personality is probably set from birth. Environmental factors can influence predispositions and traits as well. When a parent expects the recluse child to eat at the table with the family each night, it may be an environmental override for what that specific kid is predisposed to do—but the natural predispositions of the future chef require almost no external intervention when it comes to domestic expectations. On yet another hand, getting the sporty kid to sit still and read a book may be a required override of his natural disposition. If he cannot learn to sit still and read and study when he's young, he will be ill-prepared for future success.

Consequently, the parents (and the rest of society as the children leave the home) tweak each child's natural tendencies to get them to fit within normal social parameters. This is done for the safety, security, and success of both the individual and the society.

I think that as social species, dogs and humans are quite similar in many ways. Dogs are each born with a unique personality plus a capacity to be socialized and remain social in a family structure. Each breed has some general tendencies, but individuals within a breed still vary. Some pups are born gregarious and others are aloof.

In my experience working with dogs and their people, I have found that folks often err in the upbringing of their puppies by assuming that the pup's behavior defines the dog (as in, they think it is the dog's innate personality). Therefore, they feel helpless to intervene and simply accept behavior that they would never tolerate from a human child. In contrast, I examine the dog's behavior regardless of the personality. I recognize that I have a right and a responsibility to change certain behaviors, since it's my job to continue the social programming that the pup's dam and breeder started. I am responsible to impose my will upon him, at times, to set standards for behavior that will make the dog a well-adjusted social member of the family.

A pup's behavior is not who he is; it's just his behavior; it doesn't define his personality—although an individual's personality may influence his behavior. It doesn't matter what personality a kid or dog has when it behaves in an antisocial manner. It must get feedback about the behavior. When the behavior is unacceptable or antisocial, it must be overridden by a higher-ranking authority figure.

To me, personality traits are things like *thoughtful, pensive, fearless, gregarious, creative, biddable, desire to work independently, openness to change, work drive, aloofness,* or *willingness to partner with a human.* There are also behaviors that we have enhanced in specific breeds through artificial selection, such as heel nipping in herding dogs, howling in hounds, carrying objects in retrievers, or killing small animals in terriers.

The value in selecting the right breed for your lifestyle is that you can choose to spend your time with a "bookworm," a "sporty," or a "domestic kid" rather than having to adjust your lifestyle to accommodate a dog's unique disposition. I do understand that we sometimes end up having to offer a room to a niece because she lost her apartment, or we feel compelled to open our home to a neighbor fallen on tough times. Many people prefer to take in a dog, any dog, regardless of its disposition or learned manners. In those cases, we may need to adjust our standards to accommodate a dog's inherent personality. When that happens, it's important to acknowledge that a Basset Hound may have physical and intellectual traits that challenge you as a dog owner. You can't turn him into a Rottweiler!

Let's discuss some other differences between breeds. Some are easy to groom, while others require professional intervention for optimal coat care. Some breeds slobber (and by that, I am suggesting that slime may dangle from your chandelier). And then there are the size variations between breeds—which can weigh from as little as two pounds to well over two hundred. Purebred dogs can offer a near limitless array of partnerships that range from perfect lapdog to skijoring buddy to search-and-rescue partner. Understanding what makes a dog tick can lead to the best decision both for you and your happiness and the dog's well-being and contentment.

In the twenty-five years I've been working with dogs and their owners, I have seen more and more people who seem to be against the concept of purebreds. I can only guess that this is due to ignorance, because it doesn't make sense to me. A dog from a reputable, dedicated, professional breeder can be exactly what you expect in the breed of your choice. A German Shepherd Dog is not the same as a Husky, and a Golden Retriever is quite different from a Maltese. A Dachshund is not even close to presenting the qualities of a Scottish Deerhound.

A friend asked me to help her select her next dog. I discussed the vast array of breed types, but she said, "I just want a dog." To me, that is like being offered an extensive menu at a great restaurant and replying, "I just want some food."

I also want to be clear that I don't disapprove of mixed breeds. The first dog I trained was a mutt of completely unknown heritage. He was a wonderful, kind, and loyal dog that taught me many things about good management and proper training as well as unconditional love and devotion. If it weren't for him, I would never have enrolled in my first obedience class. He persevered to please me, even when I made terrible mistakes, and he was friendly and good-natured.

However, when I got my second dog, I had a specific

intention in mind: for it to compete in a sport with me. So I selected a breed and a breeder who helped me to acquire a dog with the right qualities. It can be valuable to know the heritable background of a dog if you want to partner with it in a specific way. If you select a dog of unknown heritage, you must be more resilient and accommodating to differences in the dog's character. That can be easy for some people but a complete deal breaker for others.

If you choose a mix intentionally, I strongly suggest that you research the basic qualities of the parent breeds. Crossing two breeds that have conflicting motivations can result in a dog that doesn't really know his purpose. Perhaps he'll even experience conflicting impulses. Imagine if a dog's mother is designed to kill vermin, and she is crossed with a male designed to protect livestock. When it encounters a baby duckling, does it ask, "Should I kill it or save it?"

And then there is the quagmire I call "rescue." I speculate that about 80 percent of our clients refer to their dogs that way. Curiously, it is often used to describe dogs that have merely been rehomed. An example might be, "Erma is a rescue. Our neighbor was going to move, so we took her." I suppose that can be considered a "rescue" situation, even if Erma was well maintained, loved, socialized, taken to the kid's soccer games, and attended a couple of dog-training classes when she was younger. But Bella could also be a rescue. She might have been taken from her litter at five weeks old, left in a crate for twenty hours a day, forced to urinate in her sleeping area, fed the lowest quality food, and never allowed to run around in a yard.

Most people want to claim that they rescued a dog, but very few really want a dog like Bella who truly needs to be *rescued* (not just rehomed, but saved both psychologically and physically). In fact, many rescue "organizations" refuse to take dogs like Bella because they know that she is a very bad risk.

The Bellas of the world rarely get rescued (as in saved and mended). This is because it is very challenging to truly rescue such a dog. Puppies that are removed from their litter at five weeks of age are at a huge disadvantage because they miss some critical early-life socialization that helps them to behave normally under certain situations. Dogs that are forced to mess where they sleep become what I refer to as "dirty dogs." They lose their natural inclination to stay clean. If you have ever had to manage a "dirty dog" and deal with a swooshing tail of urine-soaked feces every time you interact with the pup, it can be very nerve-racking. That's why people "rescue" dogs like Erma—they get to claim they rescued a dog, but they don't have to actually do it. Even dog-rescue organizations that take donations often fail to rescue dogs like Bella.

I must say that I don't mean that anyone should feel obligated to rescue the Bellas of the world. In fact, most people are ill equipped to take on such a project, and to do so could lead to despair and failure. The rescue organizations have already figured that out. It is about resources, and the few who could take on the rehabilitation of Bella may not have the resources to do so. Neither should they be expected to do it just because they can be successful. Life is short, and there are only so many minutes in a day. If you are rehabilitating Bella, you are not hanging out with your own dog, and your own pet suffers. I know this because I have been there more than once.

Yet, someone—we'll call him Joe—will read this, and he (or his ego) will think that I mean he must now rescue a Bella. He does not have the wherewithal, the experience, or the resources to do it, but still, he does it anyway. Then, after many months of challenges—Bella bites his little daughter and forces his wife to retreat to another room at night to avoid all the Bella drama in the house—he calls a professional dog trainer for help. We can help Bella, but we know that we cannot help Joe. Bella needs more than Joe has to offer. We have to be blunt and emphasize that Bella has bitten his daughter, because he doesn't seem to think it's all that bad: "Well, Bella is a rescue, and she has some issues."

I believe some people may "rescue" dogs because they want to feel good about it. That is the *primary* motivator. They hear over and over and over again that giving a homeless dog a chance is the "right" thing to do. However, I believe that this chorus supports a terrible situation that plagues our country—that of the unethical "backyard" breeder or puppy mill. This industry exists because people are willing to purchase the mistakes of these villains (including through rescue organizations, because "adoption" is a sale). This encourages the unscrupulous puppy producers to breed yet another litter.

You don't have to purchase a product directly from a producer to support a business. If you can appreciate the value of purchasing "cage free" eggs as it relates to animal care, you should be able to relate the same to acquiring a puppy. Do you find it acceptable to support those who produce puppies in substandard conditions, even if you don't ever see those people? In the past five years, there has been a dramatic increase in shelf space dedicated to cage-free and organic eggs. This means that producers of "factory-farmed" eggs, with hens confined to small spaces, are losing business—because the stores have not increased their total space for eggs.

I've never seen the effect of all this at the actual farm level, but I understand the theory of supply and demand. People demand eggs produced under higher standards, and the market is adjusting to expectations. There is no reason that the same thing cannot happen with dogs.

If people became interested only in puppies and dogs from reputable origins, the puppy mills would have to decide how to dispose of all their extra puppies that nobody wants. Let's aspire to a standard of verifying the actual source of birth, not just how "nice" the people (or rescue) are who offer the dogs. When demand drops, dodgy breeders will need to find another way to make a living. It sounds callous and simple—and it is both.

If it is important to you to know who produced the food you eat and feed to your family, shouldn't it be as important for you to know who produced your puppy? Shouldn't you support breeders who take the endeavor seriously and adhere to professional standards? When selecting your next dog, I encourage you to devote at least as much time and energy as you dedicate to selecting your next cartful of groceries. Toss out the notion to "rescue" your next dog, and replace it with the mantra, "know your breeder." It will make the world a better place.

I understand that this may be a politically incorrect area to tromp. But at times, it's important to step away from conventionality and advocate for the dogs. Acquiring the wrong dog is one of the ten most common mistakes that dog owners make. All the stories about Bella and Joe I have heard in the past fifteen years prove that.

Deciding on a dog, especially if you will be bringing it into a home with children, needs to be done with great care. You must do research and gather information—patiently and carefully. Your judgment must not be hurried. If you are not equipped to handle a messy project, then rescuing a dog may not be the right option for you—regardless of how it makes you feel to shout out to the world that you did.

"This is Sadie—she's a rescue!"
"This is Baron—he's a rescue!"
"This is Spike—he's a rescue!"
"This is Elsa—he's a rescue!"

Let's get off the rescue wagon and back to the concept of choosing the wrong known-bred or mix dog. Selecting the right dog for your situation is on my top-ten list because I believe it has a huge influence on whether or not you develop a successful relationship. Imagine if as a business owner, you failed to hire the right people. Would you hire a color-blind person to develop paint hues or someone who doesn't speak English to edit your American website? There's nothing wrong with a person who doesn't speak English—but she's just not the right person for that specific job. What would be worse is if you hired someone you feared.

Many people can learn to adjust to the various nuances that different breeds present. However, when the owner is afraid of his dog, things can get dangerous.

I receive dozens of e-mails from folks asking for assistance. To be honest, I know they are usually hoping for some free advice, because they live a thousand miles away and there's really no chance they will ever become a genuine client. Still, I try to help if I can.

The thing about asking for free advice, however, is that you are going to get it. Below is an actual e-mail exchange. The inquirer had read a post on my website about puppies that bite, in which I described giving the pup a quick poke with a stiffened finger around the neck area to emulate a nip from a mother dog.

QUESTION: I recently read your response to Rules for New Puppies. I'm afraid to do the poke method to correct bad behavior because I have a pit bull, and I feel that she will turn on me or get more aggressive. She is almost three months old. Do you have any input on this? It would be greatly appreciated because I'm now considering giving her up because of her bad behavior.

ANSWER: One of the most common root causes of aggressive or antisocial dogs is owners who fear them. We can usually rehabilitate an antisocial or aggressive dog, but we cannot always change the owner's perception of the dog once the owner is afraid of it. It is a recipe for disaster. If you are already afraid of a little baby three-month-old puppy, I would strongly advise either a 180-degree shift in your perception of the dog, or to rehome it immediately with someone who does not have fear of the puppy's breed.

It is not just pit bulls that face this unsettling situation. It is common in the giant breeds, such as Mastiffs, as well. People see that big dog and become concerned about its potential power. The dog senses fear from its owner or other humans and doesn't know how to process that information. So, in response, it lets out a "woof" to try to ward off those weird feelings that it senses. The "woof" is then perceived by the fearful owner that the dog is, in fact, potentially aggressive. So, she responds with more unbalanced energy back toward the dog (fear, worry, panic, some type of frantic energy).

The dog has been developed by man to subordinate itself to and work for people. Sensing apprehension or fear from the human makes the dog believe the world is a very odd, unpredictable place. It makes no sense to the dog that the higher-ranking one is afraid of him, especially a baby puppy. So, he may take control of the situation with a bite-first-ask-questions-later approach.

To me, a dog that has an owner who is afraid of it is like having a boss who is afraid of you (even though you have no plans or desires to override his authority). Worse, it's like a parent fearing his or her own child. Perceiving that a parent fears him or her doesn't add up to a child who has an inherent desire to obey authority. It causes issues that would otherwise not present themselves.

Regardless of breed, the human owner should be able to touch the dog anywhere, anytime, for any reason, and the pup should simply tolerate that. That is "normal." People with feelings such as those you suggest in your e-mail are the ones who create unbalanced, aggressive dogs out of otherwise normal, social pit-bull puppies.

If you do not change your attitude, you have a fairly big chance of raising a very antisocial puppy. But, your puppy was not born antisocial. She will become that way because of your interactions with her. Do not put the puppy's breed higher in priority than her species. She is a dog. She is three months old. While she has sharp baby teeth, and obviously she is not getting feedback from her owner about self-restraint and how to keep her teeth off human flesh, she has no malice and no drive to be aggressive at that age.

Puppies that age need someone to care for them with a high level of management. She just has a lack of understanding about the rules that you are responsible to impose upon her in "dog language" about her actions. She is treating you like another puppy, and almost all puppies play with each other using their teeth. They are not aggressive. They are puppies.

If you do not correct a puppy properly, it can perceive you as a playmate and it will come back with another nip. That is what "equals" do. You cannot be her equal. You must assume the role of "parent," "top dog," "leader," "higher-ranking one," or however you want to perceive it. She cannot learn what is acceptable if you do not teach her. If you are afraid of her or her behavior (which, to me, is the same thing), then you won't be very convincing in your role.

Either rehome her or take control. She is a baby puppy, not an alligator. Remain calm, give her a firm correction with the right attitude (cool confidence), follow the information in my article, and teach your puppy to respect you.

Also, limit the amount of free time she has so that she does not get sleep deprived (which can cause tantrums). Feed her properly. Do not interact with her in ways that hype her up (a very common mistake that puppy owners make). Make certain that she is getting enough uninterrupted sleep. Let her be a puppy. Do not let her put her teeth on you, even in play. If you have another well-balanced dog with whom she can play puppy games, that would be great too.

I do not understand why people who are afraid of pit bulls acquire them. You cannot walk on eggshells around a dog for the next fourteen years without expecting something disastrous to happen. You are either going to own your dog or you are going to have a dog that you do not trust. Make a choice.

Obviously, I am passionate about the idea that dog owners have a significant obligation to make sound, informed, and intelligent decisions about what sort of dog they acquire. Before anything else, that decision establishes the ease—or challenges—you will face with your new dog. You can't choose your relatives. You can't always decide who will work next to you at your job, but you can do the research about what sort of dog you bring into your life, and, even more important, what sort of breeder to acquire it from.

4
Beyond the Top Ten

When you write a book, it's very challenging to stick to your chosen scope. I began by creating a list of dog-owner mistakes, but it got very long. Each new mistake I listed reminded me of another. Organizing by tens seemed natural, so I chose to discuss the ten most common mistakes. Yet, there are a few more items worth mentioning briefly:

A. **If it doesn't make sense, don't do it**.

This should be everyone's mantra about almost every decision. It is especially true when you evaluate methods of dog training, even if your instructor says she has a string of letters after her name and tells you to do something in the name of science.

Sylvia and her nine-year-old daughter brought their ten-month-old Labrador Retriever, Jake, for basic training. Sylvia explained the issues they'd been having and said, "The other trainer just told us to turn around and walk away when he jumped up, but that didn't work." Then she turned to her little girl. "Stand up, Katie, and turn around. Let me show Miss Tammie what Jake did to you."

The girl got up and turned around, and her mother lifted Katie's shirt. From just above her shoulder blades to down past the waistband of her shorts, there were deep, red scratch marks. I gasped.

"Yeah—right?" Sylvia said to me. "You tell me that is good dog training!"

Humans are an intuitive species, even though many of us have lost touch with that most critical attribute. I acknowledge that much of our success comes from learning from others. However, if a "certified" dog professional tells you to ignore your dog as he jumps on your kid, leaving drag marks down her skin, I think you can toss science out the window and go with your gut.

I am aware of studies that demonstrate an animal will cease performing a behavior when he finds no reward in doing it. However, dogs can be really persistent, and people can find it impossible to *completely* ignore a dog that is causing a child to exclaim, "Mommy, it hurts!"

As a possible resolution to unruly behavior, I sometimes propose the ignoring technique too. For example, a dog that is carrying on in his crate should not be permitted out until he demonstrates self-restraint. The first few times, it can take the dog a long while to relax, especially if he has been allowed to bust out of the door for weeks or months.

I often suggest placing a chair next to the crate. The owner should face perpendicular to the dog. It allows him or her to relax and truly ignore the dog while waiting for it to stop whining, spinning, or otherwise displaying unacceptable behavior. With the ignoring technique, if the owner is committed to *figuratively* turn his or her back on the dog, a light bulb often switches on and the dog learns to show patience. This can be a powerful method of communicating expectations.

However, the first time you are late for work and don't wait for the dog to wholly relax before letting him out of the crate, he may begin to fuss again when you arrive to let him out. The *method* doesn't correct the bad behavior. It relies on the power of the owner to disregard the dog until it settles down so that the dog learns to relax.

The science behind the concept requires that the dog be *completely* ignored. But we humans are not perfect. Sometimes we speak to the dog, which is not the same as ignoring him. Situations can arise that force us to prioritize the dog's training lower than another significant event, like tending to a sick child. In my experience, it can be extremely challenging to *absolutely* ignore an unruly dog. Even I find it difficult. Simply projecting frustration energy can alert a dog that we are not truly overlooking their antics. That leads to more fussing.

As challenging as it is to alter a *crated* dog's behavior through the "ignore" method, I would never ask someone to turn a back on a *jumping* dog. It just doesn't make sense. As a dog owner, it's important to evaluate the suggestions of a professional and to choose whether they are sensible.

This philosophy holds true even if you are not working with a professional. Evaluating your own actions toward your wayward pup should be an early step in determining whether a change is necessary. If what you are doing doesn't seem reasonable, change what you are doing. Use your intuition. Be courageous. It's your dog.

B. **Get quiet.**

The notion that we are supposed to use our tone of voice to control a dog can lead their owners to squeak, squeal, or chirp continually at them. Since dogs are not a highly verbal species, I can only imagine how easy it would be for them to completely disregard all that gibberish. When we teach dogs the meanings of words, we are asking them to perform outside their natural tendencies. For that reason, any verbal information beyond the simple command word or words probably creates more confusion, rather than supports communication.

I suggest that you use simple words, speak in a calm tone, and reinforce your expectations through physical touch. That is what dogs do with each other and therefore what they expect. All those long sentences you utter simply confuse your pup.

C. **Time does not change a dog's behavior.**

"He's only two years old. He'll grow out of it."
Not.
The passage of time allows bad habits to become really bad ones. Set standards early. Pay attention. Give a warning, and then correct your dog if he begins to present the behavior you find unacceptable. Don't be lazy—do the work.

D. **Offer your dog mental and social exercise as well as physical.**

It is important to offer your dog sufficient exercise, but don't think that exercise alone will change a dog's behavior. It supplies physical activity and sometimes tires out your dog. Keeping a dog exhausted can be a lazy way to tolerate an active canine. In time, though, he will become resilient to that level of activity, and you will need to constantly increase the exercise to wear him out!

Dogs need more than just physical workouts. Regardless of her size or disposition, there are tricks and tasks that you can train your dog to perform. These may seem like mere frivolity, but if you take them seriously and set high standards for their execution, your dog will feel fulfilled and purposeful.

The feat of lying down and staying, regardless of the distraction, is "work" for any dog. During this "work," do not give him a bone to chew or allow him to saunter off and get a drink of water. He can be told to stay on a comfy dog bed. However, if you tell him to lie down, you must pay attention and correct him if he begins to break the command. While this may not seem a terribly challenging mission, it is still labor, and your dog will feel that you have high expectations for him. It will help him to realize that you value him in the pack and hold him to standards so that he can please you.

You may also train your dog to perform parlor tricks. A fun game employs the dog's natural ability to discriminate different scents, find them, and alert you to them. A quick search for "canine nose work" should get you on the right track.

Many dogs can learn to discriminate various objects (also known as toys) by name. Asking your dog to "go get the blue ball" and to refrain from picking up the "squeaky frog" or the "fuzzy mouse" can increase the importance of the game. Take your time and make it easy by playing with just one object at a time, saying its name frequently during the fun.

If you are active, take your dog to a playground when no children are there. Introduce your dog to the various obstacles (like a small slide or wobbly bridge). Or do a search for "homemade agility obstacles" and make your own equipment for your basement or backyard. If you want to be more serious about it, join an agility club.

Always consider the heritable drives that your specific dog may have. Granting her the chance to experience those instincts can be exciting for you and your pup. There are thousands of dog clubs that offer recreations from basic obedience to retriever hunting, terrier earth trials, carting, sight-hound races, sled-dog competitions, therapy-dog work, search and rescue, and even freestyle dancing (look that up and watch a few videos to get completely hooked)! Failing to provide a dog the challenge that enhances his social skills and his inherent motivations to do work is a very common mistake that dog owners make. Accomplishing the goal can be life altering and exhilarating for owner and dog, but it can be nearly impossible to do any of that fun stuff with a poorly behaved, antisocial dog.

5
Wrap It Up

There are dozens of other frequent mistakes that dog owners make. Many are even more commonplace than those I have provided here. They revolve around basic care, like not providing the highest quality nutrition you can afford for your dog or attending routine veterinary visits. Do not overlook routine grooming like nail trims, brushing, and bathing. They are all necessary. As a professional who has worked with dogs and their people for a few decades, I have focused my attention here on the issues that I feel generate the most psychological grief for dogs. Dogs don't have a voice, so I feel compelled to advocate for them the best that I can.

I fret for dogs with owners who do not honor them as members of a unique species that deserve husbandry consistent with their needs. I believe that too many people smother their dogs with what they believe is love but that is really only smothering. I hope that my words have provided a refreshing look at the best relationship you can create with your dog. In turn, I hope it leads to more happy dogs in the world.

I don't want my insistence that dog owners should be consistent, correct antisocial behavior, and refrain from coddling to be confused with a less-than-loving connection with their dogs. I often tell people that it takes truly deep devotion, love, and commitment to be willing to do the tough stuff, and I believe it. And, I think dogs sense it. Just like with humans, the ones that demonstrate the highest level of self-discipline are often those who live the most exciting lives. If you want to give your dog the best life possible, give him the benefit of being a well-mannered, trustworthy companion so that it feels effortless to engage in sports or travel with him.

I have lived with highly intelligent dogs for most of my life. They are not just stuffed animals. They are complicated individuals that seek understanding, compassion, and benevolent leadership. I think they ponder. I know they are sometimes perplexed. I have felt their desire to communicate with me. They deserve the best possible existence that I can afford them.

Dog ownership isn't about getting a nice collar and leash and taking a stroll around the block once a day, it's about developing a relationship with a member of a different species. That's pretty profound, if you think about it. You will be best served if you use all your aptitudes to interact with and influence your dog. Communication isn't about shouting out commands and making a dog behave. It is about developing an open exchange of information with an animal that doesn't speak your language but aches to partner with you, honor and respect you, and, in turn, reap the benefits of membership in your community.

Sometimes the best answer is going to come from your gut, not a book or a video. As you create a strong, predictable, reliable relationship with your dog, it will become easier to believe in your own intuition. But until then, believe anyway.

The partnership you forge with your dog may let you grow in ways you would not otherwise. To be the best leader for your dog, one of the most important talents you must cultivate is calm, confident presence. That talent will not be wasted on Fido. Learning how to present authority without a need to be domineering will help you in your relationships with family and friends, and it could even jump-start a new career or hobby.

I don't think that dogs are a mere coincidence of our human experience. The best part about practicing leadership skills with your dog is that he won't criticize your mistakes. Dogs can be incredibly tolerant of our errors, but that should be the reason that we strive to become better owners and people.

Clearly, I can't cover every possible mistake in this book. Drawing from my experience, my perspective is that it's not hard to love our dogs, but it can be hard to make them feel our love in the ways that they require. When a dog acts naughty, he is probably trying to communicate that something is amiss—with you, not him. In this book, I have given you information that I believe will enhance your relationship with your dog and afford him what he needs to be the best dog possible. In turn, he will consider you the best possible dog owner! That is what I hope for you.

Appendix A: Training Tools

I've given thorough descriptions and illustrations of the various leash and collar options in *Dog Training & Tricks: The Guide to Raising and Showing a Well-Behaved Dog*.

Please note: A training collar used properly should not be required after the first few weeks of training. If it is used as a restraint device and the dog is allowed to pull against it, it will lose its effectiveness. Take great care to keep this from happening!

The dog should not feel the collar unless the handler is delivering a quick correction that is above the threshold needed to change behavior. The lead should always be loose unless it is being used to access the collar to deliver a correction. If the collar is used appropriately, with a warning word before a correction, the dog will learn to adhere to the handler's verbal commands and no longer require physical corrections, acting in a self-restrained manner.

Appendix B: Training Methods

Leash Breaking

(from *Dog Training & Tricks: The Guide to Raising and Showing a Well-Behaved Dog*)

Communicating proactively is key to successfully using the Social Compliance Method. A dog that is just *thinking* about chasing a cat is easier to influence than a dog that is in a full-blown gallop toward the feline. The actual physical intervention needs to be significantly less intense when the dog is in the precursory stage of intention. Intervening early is better for the handler and the dog.

Before you can use a leash to access a dog's collar during training, you must teach the dog how to remain respectful on the leash. That means two things. First, the dog must not pull against the lead to move toward an object of his affection, such as food on the floor or a cat he would love to chase. Second, he must not retreat, balk, or rear up in an attempt to escape your influence. The dog must learn that he should remain calm under the umbrella of your authority.

This is where a high-quality correction collar, such as the Herm Sprenger prong collar, is valuable. If your dog is a very strong puller, avoid becoming tense, stiffening your arm and hand around the lead, or applying excessive force to counteract his pulling behavior. Remaining calm throughout the exercise is critical.

1. Position the collar high on the dog's neck so that it nearly touches his ears (remove all extra links that would allow it to slip down his neck).
2. Connect a four- to six-foot lead to the collar.
3. Remain completely calm and relaxed.

4. As the dog moves toward the end of the lead, allow him to feel the impact of the collar. If he is moving fast toward the end of the lead, stand still and hold the lead firm. This will deliver the appropriate correction for the dog's infraction. If he is moving slowly and he gently begins pulling, give a quick tug on the lead just as he reaches the end of the lead, then immediately release tension.
5. If the collar correction was sufficient, your dog will not pull again in that situation.
6. If the collar correction was insufficient, your dog may attempt to pull again. Repeat the exercise but increase the level of correction. Avoid a nagging and dragging action. Use a quick, on-off tug of the collar to emulate the rapid and nippy snap that one dog gives to another.
7. Begin to walk very slowly. This can excite the dog to race to the end of the lead again. If he is moving fast toward the end of the lead, stand still and hold the lead firm. It will deliver the appropriate correction when the dog reaches the end. If he is moving slowly and he gently starts pulling on the collar, give a quick tug of the lead and immediately release tension.
8. Remain calm and allow the collar to do the work of correction.

I cannot stress enough that the handler's attitude and presence will have a significant bearing on how well the dog responds to a correction. Some dogs will yelp or otherwise protest when they find they are no longer in charge of the direction and speed of travel. Ignoring the objection is critical. Do not let the dog use an objection to his advantage and unnerve you.

While dogs can change their behavior upon receiving

a single, good correction, most dogs do not immediately understand our overall expectations. A dog can learn not to pull on the lead in the garage, but once you walk onto the driveway, she may challenge the rule. She may learn to walk properly on the lead from the front door to the car door but may still attempt to race off when you get to the park. Once you set standards for overall performance in several different scenarios, your dog will begin to understand your general expectations. It is important to practice in a variety of settings at different times and with different levels of distraction to teach your dog that you have zero tolerance for pulling on the lead.

When your dog understands that resisting the lead will no longer be tolerated, it is time to use the same method to actively teach her the meaning of warning words. There is no need to provide any verbal cues about pulling on the lead. It is a behavior that should never be tolerated. We can use the Social Compliance Method to teach dogs the meaning of words that set expectations about limits for behavior.

Stay in a Sit Position

(from Dog Training & Tricks: The Guide to Raising and Showing a Well-Behaved Dog)

The most basic command is "sit." Many people successfully teach their dogs to assume a sitting position quite easily using a luring method. Nearly as many people complain that although their dog will sit, he will not stay.

The traditional separation of the two commands ("sit" and "stay") may explain why so many people fail to achieve their goal. In reality, there are few instances when "sit" does not mean stay sitting. When I teach a dog to sit, I do not typically use the word "stay." The dog learns that when instructed to sit, she should stay there until directed to do something else.

However, if you enter an obedience competition, you will find that the two commands are considered distinct. The judge will instruct you to sit your dog and then leave your dog. When you leave your dog (whether in a group sit exercise or to move away during the recall exercise), you will be permitted to tell her "stay." Curiously, if upon the "sit your dog" command, your dog sits and springs right back up again, the judge will not be able to continue the exercise until you get your dog sitting again. Even though there is a distinction between the "sit" and "stay" commands in competition, there is an assumption that once a dog is instructed to sit, she will remain there.

In basic training, to make things simple, let's assume that when you tell your dog to sit, lie down, or stand, you mean that he should stay in that position. Therefore, you must give that information to your dog.

Let's also assume that your dog does not know to stay unless you teach him that expectation. This will be the fairest way to go about training your dog.

Since "sit" is such a critical command, I will explain it in the greatest of detail. For additional commands or tricks, I will give less information, since each exercise builds on the skills that both you and your dog will develop during early training.

You may want your dog to sit in front of you, or you may want your dog to sit in the heel position. The heel position will be discussed later.

If you are using a bridge word or a clicker, from this point forward, when instructed to reward your dog, insert your bridge first, then give the reward.

Sit in Front
1. Place your dog in front of you in a standing position. You may need to take a step backward to help him get up if he is already sitting.
2. Hold a treat in your right hand.
3. In a kind but firm tone of voice, say your dog's name and the command "sit."
4. Allow your dog to see the treat in your right hand. Move your right hand in a sweeping motion from below the dog's chin to above his head, keeping it centered between his eyes. Do not move it so high that he attempts to sit up or get up on his hind legs. Move it at a rate that will allow him to track its movement and move it high enough that he tilts his head backward. Then stop.
5. When your dog assumes the sitting position, deliver the reward.
6. At this early stage, if your dog springs right back up again, it is acceptable.
7. If your dog does not sit, try again. Focus on your speed and your distance from the dog's face.

Struggling with the Food Reward?

If the dog is too excited about the food, use something that is less interesting, such as a piece of dry kibble. If the dog is not interested enough, use a treat that will excite him, such as cheese, chicken, or liver treats.

The Alternate Sit Technique

If the dog needs additional help in understanding your expectation, you may use a secondary technique along with the luring method or instead of it you may gently tap or tuck the dog's rear end. Additionally, you may tug up on the dog's collar.
1. Position yourself so that the dog is on your left side rather than in front of you.
2. Hold the lead in your right hand and close to the collar.
3. Say the dog's name and the command word "sit."
4. Gently tuck the dog's rump close to the base of his tail. Do not push on his spine.
5. Along with the rump tuck, tug up on the dog's collar. Make certain that it is positioned very high on his neck.
6. Once he assumes the sit position, praise him verbally. You may deliver a treat, as long as you do so while he is still sitting.

Practice
1. Repeat the exercise several times over a few days until your dog is routinely sitting.
2. Begin removing the reward (treat or toy) over time.
3. Continue to provide verbal praise each time your dog sits.
4. Initially, remove about every tenth treat, then every fifth treat, then every other treat.
5. Mix up the frequency of treat delivery, since some

dogs can learn to count!

Setting the Standard—"Sit" Means Stay

1. Once your dog demonstrates an understanding of the "sit" command, which should not take more than a few days, it's time to explain that "sit" means "stay there until I release you."
2. Adjust your dog's collar so that it is very high on his neck.
3. Put your lead in your left hand and hold it so there is very little slack. Avoid putting tension on your dog's neck.
4. Sit your dog by saying the dog's name and the word "sit."
5. Do not give the dog a treat at this time.
6. Watch your dog intently but do not become tense in body or mind. Do not allow him to get up out of the sitting position.
7. Stay close to your dog.
8. If you perceive that he is about to break his sit position, tug upward on the lead. Do not get angry, frustrated, or irritated. You are simply teaching your dog about expectations that he is not yet aware of by offering feedback about his choice to get up.
9. Be proactive. Do not wait until your dog is standing before responding.
10. Do not speak. Do not repeat the "sit" command. Do not use his name. This is very important.
11. Along with the upward tug on the collar, gently touch his rump as you might have done when he first learned to sit.
12. Expect your dog to stay sitting for fifteen to thirty seconds, then calmly end the exercise. You may deliver a treat at this time, as long as he is still sitting. Immediately begin a regimen of intermittent rewards at this stage of the training.

Do not give him a treat every time.
13. Give your release word in a relaxed manner. Do not excite him with an over-the-top song of praise. That teaches him to get up out of the sit just because you are happy with his behavior.
14. Repeat the exercise and add additional sitting time before ending it.

Why You Shouldn't Chatter to Your Dog When Teaching the Sit Command

If you want your dog to learn to sit on the first command, you should not provide second, third, or fourth commands. Those additional commands will teach him that he does not have to comply with the first command. Say it once, then make it happen.

When your dog is learning, he is concentrating. Just as it's difficult for you to learn if someone is chatting at you, your dog needs quiet time to process the information you are presenting. Providing clear, concise information without added frills gives your dog the best chance to learn the lesson.

Adding Distractions

Now that your dog is sitting on command and understands that he must stay or receive an upward collar tug, begin adding distractions. Since dogs are not a highly verbal species and instead use facial gestures and body posturing to communicate, your dog would rather "listen" to your body language than your spoken words. To help him learn spoken words better, you need to make your body movements irrelevant to him. You should eventually be able to tell your dog to sit and have confidence that he will stay there while you perhaps open the door to take a package from a delivery person. You should be able to bend over to tie your shoe, clap your hands, or even do a little jig and have your dog remain sitting. If you compete in an obedience trial, your dog will have to stay sitting while you move thirty feet away for a minute or more. He must stay put even if another dog gets up and walks about in the trial arena.

To condition your dog to distractions:
1. Sit your dog (say his name and use the command word "sit").
2. Hold the lead with just enough slack that your dog does not feel tension on his neck. Keep the lead short enough that you can immediately respond to any potential movement to get up out of the sit position.
3. Take a small step to the left and expect your dog to stay. Correct with a collar check if he does not.
4. Take a couple of small steps to the right. Correct with a collar check if you perceive that your dog is about to get up.
5. Move back and forth in front of your dog. Remain calm and relaxed yet vigilant.
6. Hold the lead slightly above your dog's head so that at the slightest indication that he is considering getting up, you can provide feedback that he is to stay.
7. Move in a larger and larger arc around your dog until you can actually walk a full circle around him. You may need to gently touch his head or shoulders the first time you walk completely around him. This is just to let him know you are in contact with him, not to actually correct him. Use the leash to give an upward tug if you think he is going to get up.
8. Bend over and touch your knees or your toes. Do a jumping jack. Wave your arms over your head. Stomp your feet. Whistle. Sing. Jump around. All the while you are doing these actions, be prepared to give a collar check if your dog begins to get up.

By this time, if you have been paying attention to your dog, you will have become quite good at observing and acting proactively. Dogs have a great deal of respect for people who present themselves as highly proactive, because this is a necessary skill of a good leader. You will find that the collar tug correction will not need to be as strong as it was when you first introduced the concept to your dog. This is a good thing. If your dog continues to break the sit position, you are probably not providing information above the threshold needed to change his behavior. You are essentially nagging your dog rather than correcting him. If this is the case, you may need to adjust the collar higher on your dog's neck, use more force when actually correcting him, or deliver a more potent collar check correction. It should not take more than three or four ten- to fifteen-minute training sessions before your dog is demonstrating a high level of understanding that "sit" means sit, no matter what. If you project frustration, anger, disappointment, or frantic energy when attempting to correct your dog, the physical action will have significantly less effect than if you remain calm and composed.

Becoming Free

The next stage in teaching a reliable sit is to drop the lead. Do this in a very nonchalant manner. If you were paying good attention and preventing your dog from getting up out of the sit while you added distractions, the act of dropping the lead should not come as a surprise to your dog. If you avoided using the leash as a restraining device, letting go of it should be fairly insignificant to both you and the dog. At this stage, you may begin walking farther from the dog. Do not give additional commands. Once you have told your dog to sit, he should expect you to back up your demands without providing a second or third command.

Increase your expectations by walking farther from the dog, turning your back on him, sitting in a chair across the room, or briefly stepping out of sight. In the beginning, do this for very short periods, before moving back toward him to a point where you could pick up the lead or gently touch him on the head. The goal is to move without allowing him to get up out of the sit position. Remain as close as necessary to help your dog understand that he is still under your authority.

Appendix C: Breed Selection

Selecting the Right Breed for Your Lifestyle

As a professional dog trainer, I consider it my task to work with both the dog and the human components of the partnership. Although my husband and I put quite a bit of time, energy, and heart into rehabilitating and training dogs, a dog's behavior is ultimately a reflection of its relationship with its people. Therefore, there's really no such thing as a "trained dog" or even a "good" dog. If the dog's owner doesn't receive an education on how to maintain a dog's psychological and social balance and then achieve those goals, the dog may revert to the same naughty behavior that it presented prior to our training.

Unfortunately, when dealing with people and their dogs, I often encounter what I consider a serious mismatch. As everyone has experienced at some point in their lives, we don't all get along with everyone. Some personality types just grate on our nerves, while others we feel comfortable sharing our lives and ourselves with intimately. Dog breeds were designed for a myriad of different occupations, some of which require strong, tenacious, stubborn determination and others that demand the dog have a softer side or the desire to partner with a human. Selecting the wrong breed type for one's lifestyle can result in a decade or more of torment—much like a bad marriage—while choosing the right breed can result in what some may consider a match made in heaven.

The domestic dog is a very unique species, created by humans for humans, and, at times, in humanity's image. The unusual genetic diversity of wild wolves has been harnessed to create incredible extremes in body style and shape, coat length and type, ear set, color, and, of course, size in our domestic dogs. But the truly most important criterion that should be explored very early in the selection process for a new companion has nothing to do with appearance.

You must commit to really understanding the type of work for which a dog was originally bred. This will provide you insight into the dog's character—what makes him tick, what lifestyle he needs to be happy and comfortable in his own skin and in your home. It will reveal his character and temperament, his mental capacities, and his mind-set. It will define his body and how he will use it. Most important, it will provide essential information on how much or little he needs to partner with his humans to feel fulfilled. It will convey what sort of leader he needs his owner to be. That is the crucial part, because it sheds light on whether a dog's owner will feel comfortable living with the dog while maintaining his or her normal lifestyle.

Choosing a Breed

To assess which breed is right for you, it is important to examine your own lifestyle first. How much do you want to work at keeping your new dog happy and healthy, mentally and physically? Some breeds have very high standards for their humans and require a significant amount of time simply to keep the dog mentally content and physically fit. Others are satisfied just knowing where the food and water bowls are and recognizing that they have a soft place to sleep, demanding little in the way of partnership.

One way to examine a breed against your lifestyle is to look at two very important selection criteria that were used in developing it. To perform the job for which it was originally bred, the breed has ended up with a unique combination of *biddability* and *work drive.* This combination can provide a good measurement of the breed's character and define the resources that it may require from the owner as its leader and companion.

Biddability is a willingness to do what is asked. It is a demonstration of obedience, tractability, docility, and submission. Dogs with a high level of biddability ache to partner with their humans. They are not fulfilled without the chance to please their owners. The work for which these breeds were originally designed tends to demand cooperation with a human rather than autonomous effort. These dogs can be a challenge to keep because they expect something of their owners beyond basic maintenance like food, water, and exercise. They anticipate daily engagement with their owners, or they become quite unhappy.

Work drive (or prey drive) is a desire to pursue the challenge of a job or some kind of quarry. Some breeds have been designed with this in mind, and dogs with a strong prey drive tend to be willing to trail or chase moving objects like toys or small animals. Breeds that are known for hunting tend to have high prey drive; however, herding dogs (that do not actually hunt and kill but rather contain and control their charges) also fall into this category. The working breeds, like the Doberman Pinscher, Newfoundland, or Rottweiler may also be categorized as having high work drive. Dogs with high prey or work drive are often very good at games like retrieving or tug-of-war, which can be motivators or rewards for other activities like Schutzhund, tracking, obedience training, or Agility. On the contrary, some breeds have been designed with little or no prey drive so they can be successful at their intended jobs. These include the guardian breeds.

In general, though with many exceptions, breeds fall into one of four quadrants defined by the amount of prey or work drive versus biddability or need to please a human partner. Understanding where your desired breed falls will help you realize how much leadership, management, and daily maintenance your dog will need from you. If your personality type isn't suited for the level of leadership your "perfect" breed really needs, or if you have higher expectations for partnership than your desired breed may be able to offer, you may want to rethink your decision. Hopefully, you will have your dog for twelve or more years, so making a good assessment before you acquire your new puppy can have an impact on the next decade or more of your life!

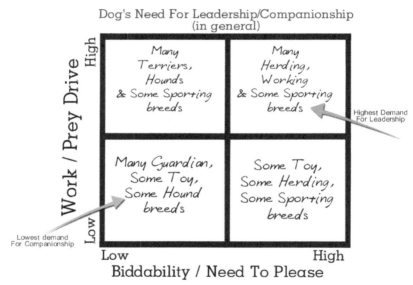

Low Prey Drive/ Low Biddability

Breeds that fall into the low-prey-drive and low-biddability quadrant tend to be fairly easy keepers. They do not want to kill your cat or chase children on bicycles, and they are not all that concerned about the effort you put into being their leader. There are massive breeds and diminutive breeds that fall into this category. The livestock-guardian breeds, like the Great Pyrenees, have little desire to chase after small animals. Instead, they take ownership of them and guard them from outside threats. A Great Pyrenees that presents with too much prey drive could end up chasing and even killing the baby lambs that it was designed to defend. This is the difference between guarding work and prey-driven tasks (such as hunting). The livestock-guardian breeds have a good work ethic, but it will not be displayed as a willingness to partner and do activities with humans. They are not highly biddable, preferring to work autonomously. Also in the low-prey-drive /low-need-to-please category are some of the toy breeds. The Pekingese, for example, is a fairly independent breed that has little need to please its owner, but it also does not have a high prey drive.

High Prey Drive/Low Biddability

Scent hounds, sight hounds, and terriers tend to fall into the category of high prey drive but low biddability. They can perform the jobs for which they were originally designed without much intervention or guidance from their human leader. When a Beagle gets onto the trail of a rabbit, he does not turn back to his human and say, "Hey, I've found a rabbit trail. Shall I follow it for you, master?" No, the Beagle simply follows the trail and feels its full sense of happiness with or without human approval.

Low biddability does not imply that the dogs do not enjoy human companionship; they just don't have a high need for a leader. Dogs in this category are often considered stubborn, but they simply do not need to please their humans to feel good about themselves. It takes a certain personality to love these breeds. The hounds tend to make exceptional companions for people who enjoy the company of a dog but don't have a lot of time for sophisticated training. These dogs still need proper management (hounds should have the freedom to run and explore in a well-fenced area) but their owners don't have to offer a lot of training or daily mental exercises.

Terriers have a tenacity and willful spirit that is highly entertaining until their owners expect them to do something other than what they choose to do! This is not to say that they don't benefit from clear boundaries and limits for their behavior or require appropriate training and exercise for their size and activity level. All breeds do. However, the challenge of changing a terrier's view on life may require more resolve than the dog—or its person—possesses. It can be quite taxing for some people and nearly impossible for others.

Low Prey Drive/High Biddability

Breeds with high biddability but low prey or work drive typically make wonderful companions and entertaining pets. These dogs have no need to do highly sophisticated jobs, but they have very high affinity for their humans. They are usually easy to train. They need people. Although they don't need a high-powered job to be happy, they do enjoy partnering with their humans toward some type of goal.

Many breeds that were originally designed for fairly challenging jobs but have now been bred for decades as show dogs or pets often fall into this category. The Collie and the Golden Retriever come to mind. Many such dogs no longer herd or hunt but instead have been bred as companion animals. Selective breeding as companion animals (only) has also bred out the original high prey or work drive, yet their desire to please remains high.

Many toy breeds also fall into this category, as they have often been bred as companions for centuries, without selection for work that would require high prey drive. A breed with a low prey drive and high biddability may be just the right dog for someone who would rather not work so hard to provide his or her pet with a hobby but who enjoys a dog that wants to interact.

High Prey or Work Drive/High Biddability

The dogs that top the scale in both work or prey drive and need to please are usually intelligent breeds that still perform the job for which they were bred, or an offshoot of that work. Many herding and working breeds are in this quadrant. While intelligence and biddability are criteria that people often believe they want in their pets, the combination can result in a dog that is needier of both mental and physical exercise than most people can truly dedicate to it.

These breeds have high expectations of impeccable leadership from their owners. Their original work was often dangerous and required trust in a highly competent leader. For example, a herding dog cannot perform the job for which it was bred without a human partner. Herding work can be life threatening, especially when dealing with cows and their calves or ewes with lambs. If the shepherd errs and gives the dog the wrong command at a critical time, the dog could be killed. Therefore, these breeds often have the capacity for intelligent disobedience while maintaining a high level of compliance in all other situations. This requires a highly sophisticated canine mind—something more than an average dog owner may truly want to handle.

A dog with a strong work drive and high biddability makes an excellent companion for someone who wants to pursue an interactive sport such as Agility or search and rescue or who may use the dog for its original intended purpose (like herding). But the dog will feel lost without sound and fair leadership, so the task of owning such a breed may be daunting to many.

Making the Final Decision

When I ask my clients why they chose the breed they did, the most common response is that they knew a friend who had one and they liked that dog so well, they wanted one just like it. However, they did not analyze their daily lives versus the dog owner's lifestyle. A happy and content dog is typically also well behaved. An unhappy, unfulfilled dog often acts out and can be very destructive. To select the right dog, it is important for a new dog owner to choose a breed that will be content living within the confines of his or her existing lifestyle, and, more important, his or her leadership style.

To make a successful match, first determine your expectations for relating with and managing the dog. Do not consider specific breeds at this time; simply define your anticipated daily interactions. Do you want to train the dog to be the next Agility superstar (attending classes three times a week and practicing an hour each night)? Or do you simply want a buddy that you can take on daily walks and who will otherwise enjoy lying at your feet?

Then, identify the quadrant(s) from which your perfect companion will come. If you are interested in a specific breed, research how it fits in your quadrant(s)—or not—by reading the breed standard, exploring the breed's history, or speaking to reputable breeders. Learn its typical prey or work drive and biddability or willingness to please. Ask what sorts of activities and daily maintenance will keep the dog happy and mentally healthy.

If the breed fits your expectations, then you are ready to begin researching all the avenues to acquire a new dog or puppy. But if it does not meet your needs, then move on. There are hundreds of breeds, all with unique characters, work styles, and needs for human leadership.

Acquiring a new puppy is a very big decision and

should not be made lightly or based on inadequate selection criteria. Your dog's behavior will be a direct reflection of his psychological well-being, which is directly related to how he feels about your leadership and management. A breed that is "good" for one individual is a horror for another. Taking the time to truly understand what you want and how you can get it will be worth every moment spent in the pursuit of your next best friend.

Appendix D: Breeder Research

How to Research a Puppy Breeder

Here is a process you can follow to research specific breeders.

I start by examining the verifiable genetic health of the dogs they breed (their breeding stock). At a minimum, good breeders test for the most common heritable diseases in their breed. Except for a very tiny handful of breeds that do not seem to be plagued with hip dysplasia, most breeders test for it. In the United States, they may use the Orthopedic Foundation for Animals (OFA), PennHIP, or a report from a university veterinary school to provide evidence of their dogs' hip results. Other countries have their own systems.

There are different eye diseases in different breeds. For breeds that don't have serious problems with heritable eye conditions, no testing is performed. Other common heritable conditions that are tested for include elbow dysplasia, patellar luxation (knee problems), and thyroid or cardiac conditions. Some breeds (Doberman Pinschers, as an example) present with a bleeding disorder, and quality breeders routinely test for that.

The OFA website lists health-screen tests on the search page. Some apply just to one or a few breeds. OFA does not provide tracking or testing results on all heritable conditions, so consider the OFA website just a beginning for your research: www.ofa.org.

To determine what may be necessary testing for a specific breed:

1. Do some research on the breed's general health by visiting the breed's American Kennel Club (AKC) parent-club website (or that of another nonbiased breed organization). Go to www.akc.org, do a search of

the breed, and find the link to the parent club.

2. Once at the relevant website, look for a link to "Health and Research" or something similar, and review the breed's health conditions, current research on them, and available tests.

3. Then look for something like "Breeder Guidelines" and see if any heritable disease testing is recommended for breeders.

4. Check out the parent club's Breeder Referral as a starting point to search for a quality puppy. Breeders' websites (even for faraway ones you know you won't use) will familiarize you with what they say about their breeding dogs' health screens and performance titles.

5. Once you know what health conditions are most important to review when selecting a breeder, use the OFA website to determine a fairly accurate snapshot of your breed's general health. Go to www.ofa.org and click on "Statistics and Data."

6. Then, click on "Hip Dysplasia." At the top of the columns, click on "Breed" to find your breed's rank and statistics. At the time of this writing, the Bulldog ranked first (meaning it has the highest percentage of dysplastic dogs) with a 65 percent HD rate. English Springer Spaniels are ranked eighty-fifth out of 183 breeds, with a 13 percent HD value (the number of x-rays submitted to OFA that are scored dysplastic).[1]

7. Check other potential diseases that may be of concern in your breed by going back to "Statistics and Data" and clicking on, say, "Elbow Dysplasia."[2] Note

---

[1] The ranking by breed is a combination of percent dysplastic versus percent "excellent"-rated individuals (13.4 percent for Springer Spaniels). As a comparison, Border Collies are ranked 109 (slightly better than the ESS), with 16.7 percent excellent rated and 10.7 percent dysplastic rated. This is OFA's method of ranking breeds based on their experience with the disease. Others in the field may do a different analysis to assess the breed's health for hip conformation. Many speculate that because hip conformation is probably controlled by a number of genes, it cannot be eradicated through selective breeding.

that you may find that some breeders do not find value in testing for an uncommon condition even if a test exists.

Each breed has a unique general health status, and the potential buyer needs to assess the risk of purchasing a puppy whose parents have or have not been tested for certain conditions. Some breeders do every single test that is available (at great expense); however, they may not test their breeding stock to determine whether it can perform the work for which the breed was originally designed, or perhaps they do not work with their dogs in any performance events.

Working with a breed in its area of expertise is a good way to determine temperament in an animal, since working places stress on the dog to perform and to work with a human partner. I would rather put resources into herding with my dogs to assess their value as breeding stock than spend money to test for diseases that are uncommon in the breed and therefore of lower risk. That's my personal choice, and each breeder has an opinion on what is important when producing puppies. The buyer's responsibility is to determine whether the breeder's values regarding breeding dogs are similar to his or hers.

8. Based on the general health information at the national breed club's website, review other health conditions that may not be reported at the OFA website. Some diseases can now be confirmed using DNA markers. One company who offers tests is at www.Optigen.com. Click on "Tests" to find a list of conditions by breed name. Some DNA-marker tests are done by the university where the test was first developed; the parent club's website should have links to places that offer them.

---

[2] ESS have a 14.5 percent elbow-dysplastic rate. On the contrary, in Border Collies, elbow dysplasia is not at all common. Ranked 98 out of 123 breeds, there's a 98.4 percent normal and 1.5 percent dysplastic in BCs.

9. Once you understand which "reasonable" health screens a breeder should perform, check the breeder's website for proof of the testing.

Some breeders provide a direct link to a dog's OFA records (which allows them to see if the dog has relatives with OFA health screens as well). The OFA suggests that it is better practice to "breed dogs whose relatives have normal hips." If a breeder claims that a dog has OFA-cleared hips but doesn't provide proof on the website, go to OFA and search on the dog's official name. If the information is not there, ask to see a copy of the original result forms.

The Canine Eye Registry Foundation registers the results of eye tests by board-certified ophthalmologists. Some eye conditions are now verifiable via DNA testing, so a CERF exam is no longer as important. Knowing the dog's genotype is more valuable than knowing its phenotype, which is all that an ophthalmologist is capable of determining via a physical exam. However, a CERF test associated with a breeding dog shows that a breeder assessed an eye condition. Learn about a breed's potential eye conditions yourself (e.g., just search on "English Spaniel eye disease"). It can be very valuable information for a potential puppy buyer.

So far, you know you should review the health-screen data of any breeder's stock. You should also review the temperament and assess the quality of the potential puppy's parents.

Temperament can sometimes be evaluated via performance in breed-specific tests or trials (hunting or herding trials, for example) or general performance events (obedience or Agility competitions, or search-and-rescue certifications). Meeting the dogs or seeing them perform is also a good option.

Now let's discuss reviewing the parents' structure. A dog's structure can be based on orthopedic health screens as well as general appearance. One of the main points of a conformation event (a dog show) is to allow a judge to review the dog's overall conformation to the breed standard and make judgments based on the standard. A dog with the letters *Ch* before its name means that it is a champion—judges have chosen it as a winner in enough competitions with enough others of its breed for it to earn that title.

When assessing the quality of the actual puppy, consider the following:

1. Some health screens are performed on the puppies, not just parents. Ask the breeder to provide any documentation.

2. Temperament—this is not always easy, but a good breeder can help in this area if he or she has experience. Certainly you don't want to purchase a very shy puppy.

3. Structure—this is not always easy to do with a puppy, but a good breeder can help in this area as well, if he or she is experienced.

4. Go with your heart (once the health, structure, and temperament of the parents and puppy meet your needs). Choose the puppy that strikes your fancy.

If you like a certain color or marking pattern, go with it. Pick the puppy that makes your heart sing.

Also by Tammie Rogers

4-H Guide: Dog Training & Dog Tricks.

Dog Algebra: When Positive Reinforcement Fails to Solve the Problem

Dog Training & Tricks: The Guide to Raising and Showing a Well-Behaved Dog

About the Author

Tammie and her husband, Robert, operate DarnFar Ranch, LLC, a professional dog-training company, as well as Committed Canine, a business dedicated to the training and education of service dogs and their handlers. They reside on a rural farm in Fayette County, Illinois.

Tammie earned a degree in biology from Coe College in Cedar Rapids, Iowa, and worked as a researcher in academia and corporate America for twenty years while active in dog training and trialing. In 2001, she began to pursue dog training full time.

In 2017, Tammie put writing first and relies on Robert to spearhead their training efforts so that she can aspire to share the knowledge she has gained over the past thirty years working with dogs and their people.

Made in the USA
Middletown, DE
24 July 2020